RESPONSORIAL PSALMS OF SUNDAY

Silvester O'Flynn OFM Cap

The Responsorial Psalms of Sunday

the columba press

First published in 2006 by
the columba press
55A Spruce Avenue, Stillorgan Industrial Park,
Blackrock, Co Dublin

Cover by Bill Bolger
Origination by The Columba Press
Printed in Ireland by ColourBooks Ltd, Dublin

ISBN 1 85607 539 7

Acknowledgements
Quotations from the Psalms are taken from the Grail version, copyright © 1963 by The Grail (England), reprinted by permission of Harper-Collins Publishers Ltd..

Table of Contents

Introduction

The psalms are prayers from the time before Christ and were used in Jewish liturgies. One hundred and fifty of them were eventually collected in the Book of Psalms. Although they sometimes betray pre-Christian sentiments such as thirsting for revenge or the destruction of enemies, or lack belief in the afterlife, yet they have an enduring appeal because of their sheer humanity, always seen in the light of faith straining for God. Their poetry is grounded in an honest experience of the human condition which transcends cultural diversity, historical distance and geographical differences. What makes them so special is that this experience is always seen in a relationship with God who is both known and unknown, intimate and distant, consoling and challenging.

As a school of prayer, the psalms continue to provide us with the language of prayer. This is especially true of the lamentation psalms which provide words for times of suffering and darkness when people find it hard to pray. Saint Paul, writing to the Romans, gave a very consoling message in stating that when we do not know how to pray properly, the Spirit comes to our aid. The Book of Psalms remains one of the greatest sources of prayer provided by the Spirit.

A section of a psalm, usually no more than three or four verses, is used in the Liturgy of the Word every day at Mass. It is called the Responsorial Psalm because it is intended to be a response or echo of the first reading of the day. It picks up a pertinent theme from the reading and weaves it into a prayer. A short response is repeated by all present in a way of engaging them actively in the sacred word.

On the Sundays in Ordinary Time, the first reading itself is chosen as a preparation for the gospel of the day, so we find that the psalm, while echoing the Old Testament reading, also anticipates the gospel. Because we are more familiar with the gospel than the Old Testament, in these reflections I have tended to highlight the connection of the psalm with the gospel more than with the first reading. However, in the seasons of Advent, Christmas, Lent and Easter, since the first reading has no deliberate connection with the gospel, neither is there a thematic connection between the psalm and the gospel.

Although the psalms predate the life of Christ by several centuries, yet in the overall unity of revelation and the plan of salvation, one can glean insights into the gospel from the psalms. Various writers have compared the psalms to the water at Cana waiting for Christ to turn it into wine, or like the unconsecrated bread which is to be given new life by the power of God. Christians can often see depths of meaning far beyond the understanding of the original writer. Think, for instance, of 'The Lord is my Shepherd', or 'He has prepared a banquet for me.' This interplay of gospel and psalm ought to be of benefit to those who practise *Lectio Divina* with the Sunday gospels as they move from *meditatio* to *oratio*. The psalms give us the language of prayer. This book of reflections on the responsorial psalms is offered to all who wish to draw more sustenance for their prayer from the liturgical readings of each Sunday.

To attain the full benefit of these reflections it will be necessary to read them in conjunction with the other readings.

THE PILGRIMAGE OF LIFE
Psalm 121:1-2, 4-5, 6-9

Advent is a season of preparing for the threefold coming of Christ: his past coming which we celebrate at Christmas; his future coming at the end of life; and his everyday coming to us in personal relationship. The liturgical year begins with readings about the end of life, like reminding people about their destination before they start out on a journey. So, we hear the Lord say in today's gospel to stand ready at all times for we know not the time of his final coming.

Our life therefore is a pilgrimage towards God. The psalm of the day is the prayer of pilgrims, rejoicing to have the journey behind them as they have reached Jerusalem.

Now our feet are standing within your gates, O Jerusalem.

To the pilgrim, Jerusalem is the holy city with God's temple within its walls. It is the city chosen by David as a centre of unity among the diverse tribes.

It is there that the tribes go up, the tribes of the Lord,
there to praise the Lord's name.

David hoped that their rivalries would dissolve in the celebration of their unity as God's chosen race. Jerusalem's name is associated with *shalom*, peace. In a sad reversal, it is now the epicentre of conflict.

Psalms for the good of Jerusalem can be used as prayers for the church. As we begin the journey of a new year we pray that the church will be a source of unity and peace in the world.

May peace reign in your walls,
in your palaces, peace!

THY KINGDOM COME
Psalm 71:1-2, 7-8, 12-13,17

On the Second Sunday of Advent we are introduced to John the Baptist. There is an urgency in his exhortation to repent because, as he says, the kingdom of God is at hand. The memory of some great kings like David and Solomon imbued the people with hope that the Messiah-King would usher in a new era of justice and peace for all.

In his days justice shall flourish
and peace till the moon fails.

This psalm is a prayer for the king: that he would be given the wisdom to judge wisely and that his reign would be characterised by care for the poor and needy. Justice is one of the pillars of society, beginning with the recognition of the human rights of the poor and powerless.

Today's first reading is Isaiah's vision of a world in which all the traditional enemies live in peace together, with a little boy to lead them. Advent sets our minds towards the birth of the little boy. In time Jesus began his ministry by proclaiming that the kingdom of God was at hand. But the work begun by Jesus is far from completion. We still have hostility, divisions, wars and injustice. We have been given the king while the kingdom is still growing.

The spirituality of Advent taps into our experiences of going forward in hope. We are renewed in our prayer for an end to these evil conditions. We dream again that the wolf will lie down with the lamb. So, in Advent there is a special urgency in our prayer: Thy kingdom come.

COME AND SAVE US
Psalm 145:6-10

This psalm celebrates the unending fidelity of God's love, seeking to repair and heal rather than destroy. It is the Lord who keeps faith forever. Isaiah, in today's first reading, has an extraordinary insight into God's unfailing love.

Look your God is coming, vengeance is coming,
the retribution of God, he is coming to save you.

God's sort of vengeance is not about punishment: it involves destroying the sin but saving the sinner.

The preaching of John the Baptist tended more towards retribution as punishment. He used the images of the axe and the winnowing fan. Jesus, however, set out not to destroy, but to liberate. The apocalyptic approach of the Baptist held that things were so bad that God would have to wipe out people before starting afresh. The prophetic approach of Jesus maintained that God is here in this messy situation and he sought to fan into flame the tiniest spark of possibility. The responsorial psalm sounds like a commentary on his ministry, bringing hope and healing to the blind, the imprisoned, those bowed down, the stranger, widow and orphan.

Our faith-journey in Advent touches our experiences of winter, wilderness and waiting. The spirituality of the season is a boost to our hope. Hope is the virtue that enables faith to hold on. Hope is the conviction that someone is coming. As long as we can say 'Come', we have hope. With the psalmist we pray:

Come, Lord, and save us.

LET THE LORD ENTER
Psalm 23:1-6

This is a pilgrimage psalm. As the pilgrims went up in procession towards the house of God they praised the Lord as the creator of the world and all its wonders.

The Lord's is the earth and its fullness,
the world and all its peoples.

Then they acknowledged that to enter the house of God they must be purified of all wrongdoing.

Who shall climb the mountain of the Lord?
Who shall stand in his holy place?
The man with clean hands and pure heart.

Christians see Jesus as the sinless one who lifts up fallen humanity and cleanses our defilement. At Christmas we will celebrate the wonder of the incarnation, that the God of glory came down to the tent of our humanity. We do not have to wait to be totally perfect to climb up to God because our Saviour has come down to meet us where we are at, in our imperfect state.

The gospel of the day is about God preparing Joseph and Mary for the birth of the Lord among us. On our part, the best preparation for Christmas is to be humble enough to acknowledge our need of a Saviour. An Advent confession celebrates the cleansing of sin. The good news is that we do not have to climb up by our own efforts because the Lord has stooped down to lift us up.

Let the Lord enter! He is the king of glory.

MIDNIGHT WONDER
Psalm 95:1-3, 11-13

Some years ago, a storm of hurricane proportions left us without electric power for Christmas Midnight Mass. It was a blessing in disguise as the soft, flickering light of many candles created a more prayerful ambience. There was general disappointment when the glaring brightness of electric lights returned before the end of Mass. The special wonder of Midnight Mass has suffered because people have become accustomed to Mass at night, plus the fact that Midnight Mass is celebrated in many places some hours before midnight.

Memories come back of frosty nights and starry skies lending distance to our eyes and imagination. The incarnation is a feast for all creation. The little body grown in the womb of Mary was composed of the same substances and chemicals as the rest of creation. All things are newly sanctified in the Word made flesh.

O sing a new song to the Lord.
Sing to the Lord all the earth.

Our psalm invites the skies to rejoice, the earth to be glad, the sea and all its creatures to thunder praise. The land and its inhabitants are to rejoice and the trees must wave their arms in exultation. And all because of *the presence of the Lord, for he comes, he comes to rule the earth.*

Before he could rule us he had to become one of us. Now as our brother, one of ourselves, he sets us aright with the Father ... his justice rules the earth.

Today a saviour has been born to us;
he is Christ the Lord.

DAWN LIGHT
Psalm 96:1, 6, 11-12

The Dawn Mass takes up the theme of light. At this time of year, as winter passed the shortest day, pagans had a great celebration to honour the return of the unconquered sun. Christians saw this winter festival as the ideal time to honour the birth of Jesus, the light of the world. Luke's narrative of the nativity makes the point that the birth of Jesus occurred while shepherds kept watch through the night.

Light shines forth for the just
and joy for the upright of heart.

December's darkness is banished by glittering street lights, flickering fairy lights and warm candlelight in the window to welcome the wanderer. Our psalm catches the cosmic dimension of the celebration, calling on the earth to rejoice, the coastlands to be glad and the skies to proclaim God's glory to all peoples. The response points to the specifically Christian reason for celebration:

This day new light will shine upon the earth:
the Lord is born for us.

Paul, in the second reading, reminds us that the great news of Christmas was not something that was earned but it was 'for no reason other than his own compassion that he saved us'. We respond to God with the psalmist:

Rejoice, you just in the Lord;
give glory to his holy name.

A WONDERFUL EXCHANGE
Psalm 97:1-6

Sing a new song to the Lord
for he has worked wonders.

The theological wonder of Christmas unfortunately gets lost all too easily amidst culinary festivities and religious sentimentality. The readings at the Day Mass draw us beyond the crib to a deeper reflection on the incarnation. John's prologue reflects on the wonderful exchange in which we are the beneficiaries. At the preparation of the gifts at Mass we pray: 'By the mystery of this water and wine may we come to share in the divinity of Christ who humbled himself to share in our humanity.'

But to all who did accept him
he gave power to become children of God.

The responsorial psalm celebrates the wonders of God's work.

The Lord has made known his salvation;
has shown his justice to the nations.

The justice which Jesus brought was not about doling out punishment but about setting people at one with God. He is the one who brings salvation to all the earth. We respond in Christmas song to the Word of God. It is always a new song every time we pray.

When the Word was made flesh he brought the song of heaven down to our world. He lifts us up to participate in divine worship. It is the privilege of liturgy to participate in the eternal praise of the Father, through the Son, in the unity of the Holy Spirit. The Word of God took on our flesh so that our words of prayer might share in divine worship.

Sing a new song to the Lord
for he has worked wonders.

FAMILY LIFE
Psalm 127:1-5

Since the family is still the basic unit of society, good family life is the foundation of a stable society. In our rapidly changing society, family life is under pressure. People change jobs, addresses and partners. Houses are bigger but families are smaller. In some places more than half the births are outside of marriage. The number of single parent families has multiplied. Many mothers work outside the home, some by choice, others of necessity.

Today's psalm, although it originated in a very different culture, celebrates some of the qualities of family which belong to all times.

O blessed are those who fear the Lord
and walk in his ways.

Reverential fear of God is the beginning of wisdom. Blessed is that family where the law of God is the light which guides the way and sets the values.

By the labour of your hands you shall eat. The wholesome goodness of work is recognised. Ghandi numbered wealth without work as one of the seven sins of society. The psalm celebrates the feminine qualities which make woman the heart of the home. Then follows the picture of the children gathered at the table. Nowadays many children take their tray to the play-station rather than experience table-fellowship. This is a great pity as the family meal is one of the few occasions where all members sit down together.

Times have changed but the qualities of stable family life remain the same. May the Lord bless our families all the days of our life.

CHILDREN OF GOD
Psalm 147:12-15, 19-20

Our liturgy today advances from Christ's birth among us to our birth in Christ. John's prologue presents Jesus as the Word of creation, through whom all things came to be. He is the Word of revelation: 'The word was the true light that enlightens all.' He is the Word made flesh who dwelt among us at a particular period in history. And he is the Word of invitation, bestowing the power to become children of God to all who receive him.

The psalm of the day calls on Jerusalem (for us, read church) to praise God who has sent out his word to the earth. Paul prayed for a spirit of wisdom and perception that we might understand the rich blessings brought to us in Christ Jesus, the Word made flesh.

He has strengthened the bars of your gates. Jesus promised that the powers of the underworld would never overcome the church.

He has blessed the children within you ... recalling the gospel picture of his warm welcome to the children.

He established peace ... above all, in reconciling the sinner with God.

He feeds you with finest wheat ... in the sacred bread of Eucharist, the bread from heaven which contains all sweetness.

He makes his word known ... and this teaching is the light of life.

His laws and decrees guide us and those who walk in his light do not stumble. Blessed are they who receive his word and live as children of the Father.

LORD OF ALL NATIONS
Psalm 71:1-2, 7-8, 10-13

Epiphany means the revelation of Jesus to the world. All nations shall fall prostrate before you, O Lord. The responsorial psalm is a prayer used at the coronation of a new king: that he might bring true justice to the people, especially the poor and the needy who are helpless.

In his days justice shall flourish
and peace till the moon fails.

The psalmist predicts that foreign kings would come to pay respect to this good king. The Great River is the Euphrates on the eastern border while Tharshish and the sea coasts are to the west. Sheba and Seba represent the south. Mention of Sheba calls to mind the Queen who travelled with gifts of gold and incense in recognition of the wisdom of King Solomon. Although it is not written in the Bible, there was a tradition that her journey was guided by a star. Matthew's gospel takes this story as a template for the journey of the wise men from the East who were led by a star to bear gifts of gold, incense and myrrh, in tribute to the new-born king. The Magi represent the coming of the nations to fall prostrate before Jesus. The child of Mary belongs to the whole world.

Before him all kings shall fall prostrate,
all nations shall serve him.

Where is the star to lead people to Christ today? It must be in the living example of those who bear the name of Christian.

BELOVED CHILDREN
Psalm 28:1-4, 9-10

The celebration of the baptism of Jesus might be called Epiphany Part 2. It is the day of the revelation of Jesus as the Beloved Son of the Father. This is recognised when we reflect on it as one of the five mysteries of light in the Rosary.

The psalm chosen for the feast arises from the revelation of God's awesome power in a terrific storm. Heaving seas and thunderous roars express the mighty power of God. This God of glory is to be adored. Three times the psalm mentions *the voice of the Lord ... resounding on the waters, full of power, full of splendour.* These lines attained a new, Christological application at the baptism of Jesus, when the voice of the Father was heard over the shallow waters of the Jordan.

In his preaching, John the Baptist said that he baptised with water but that the one coming after him would baptise with the Holy Spirit. The Christian sacrament of baptism is administered not only with water but with words which invoke the name of, that is the power of, Father, Son and Holy Spirit. Once again, it is the voice of the Lord over the water, full of power, full of splendour.

At the Jordan, the voice of the Father proclaimed Jesus as his Beloved Son. The presence and power of God in the water of the sacrament invites all who are baptised to grow in the intimate relationship of being children of God.

The Lord's voice resounding on the waters,
the Lord on the immensity of waters;
the voice of the Lord, full of power,
the voice of the Lord, full of splendour.

PRAYER OF HEARTFELT SORROW
Psalm 50:3-6, 12-14, 17

On the Sundays of Lent, unlike the Sundays in Ordinary Time, the first reading does not have a direct link with the gospel. This Lent these Old Testament readings recall the stages of salvation history, beginning with the fall of Adam and Eve. This simple story is an acute observation of the subtlety of temptation and fall. The *Miserere* psalm is David's heartfelt prayer of repentance when the fog of passion dissipates and he sees his catalogue of sins. His conscience was startled by Nathan's story of the wealthy man who demanded the solitary lamb of a poor family. 'You are the man!' He recognised how wrong he had been in committing adultery, in plotting the death of Uriah and in causing many deaths in a contrived battle. But the deepest cut was the pain of having sinned against God. *Against you, you alone, have I sinned.*

The essence of sin is the offence against God . David was the man who had been given so much, yet he wanted more. 'Who could be more greedy,' asked Augustine, 'than the man for whom God is not enough?'

Though crushed and bleeding in heart, David remembers that God is full of kindness, compassion and mercy. He humbly prays for *a pure heart and a steadfast spirit*. He is confident that God will restore joy to his soul and will open his lips in praise. The ashes of Lent were a wake-up call to our consciences. Lent is a time for reflection, honest confession and the celebration of God's mercy.

THE JOURNEY OF FAITH
Psalm 32:4-5, 18-22

The second stage of salvation history is the story of Abraham whose life is a journey in faith. Trusting in God's promise he set out for the unknown on a life-journey marked by blessings and trials. Abraham is the model of what a life of faith involves. The psalm chosen to accompany his call may be regarded as a prayer for a journey.

May your love be upon us, O Lord,
as we place all our hope in you.

What a beautiful prayer! One to repeat endlessly. One of the most appealing images in the psalms pictures the light of God's face shining upon us. A face comes alive and glows in the presence of love. On the holy mountain of prayer, the face of Jesus shone like the sun for Peter, James and John. And the voice of the Father told them to listen to Jesus. Their memory of vision and voice would carry them though the dark times ahead. Just as the memory of God's promised blessing sustained Abraham in his journey of faith. We know how photographs of loved ones can sustain us in times of absence.

The psalmist draws strength from the remembrance of God's word, ever faithful and trustworthy. He visualises the face of God turned lovingly towards him.

The Lord looks on those who revere him,
on those who hope in his love.

Lent calls us to spend more time listening to God's word and beholding his face as we journey towards the holy mountain of encounter with the Easter Lord.

HARD OF HEART, HARD OF HEARING
Psalm 94:1-2, 6-9

The third stage of salvation history is the Exodus journey from Egypt to the promised land. Today's reading recalls how the people, tormented by thirst, doubted that God would provide water to satisfy their thirst. The day of rebellion was inscribed in memory for all time in the placenames, Massah meaning conflict, and Meribah meaning grumbling.

The psalm, which is an invitation to morning prayer, recalls Massah and Meribah in a note of warning not to let our hearts be hardened.

O that today you would listen to his voice!
'Harden not your hearts.'

At the well in Samaria Jesus met a woman whose heart was hardened by the religious prejudices of the time and by her personal experience of multiple infidelity. His gentle approach melted her barriers and brought her to worship in spirit and in truth.

Soil that has become as hard as rock tends to resist the water that would make it fertile again. In the miracle of God's grace, as the first reading recounts, the rock itself can become the source of saving. The psalm invites us to *come, ring out our joy ... to bow and bend low ... to kneel before the God who made us.*

Lent is a time to listen to God's word. In its light we ask ourselves if there are any doubts, conflicts or grumbling which may be hardening our hearts to God's invitation. The Lord's word is a spring from which flows the water to satisfy our deep, inner thirst. Strike the rock with the rod of faith.

THE SHEPHERD'S LIGHT
Psalm 22

Salvation history today advances to the anointing of the young shepherd, David. The psalm chosen to accompany this reading is the much loved shepherd psalm. One task of the shepherd is to be the eye of protection for the flock. Many paintings of the Good Shepherd portray him with a lantern in hand. He sees where there will be fresh pastures and restful waters. He leads them along a safe path, away from dangers. His guiding light is most powerfully appreciated in the valley of darkness. The anointing of David foreshadows the coming of Jesus Christ, the Anointed of the Father.

The granting of sight to the blind man is the second of John's stories which are used in Lent for the instruction of catechumens on their journey towards baptism at Easter. Baptism was at one time called the sacrament of illumination. Taking light from the paschal candle is still part of the ceremony. Paul, in today's second reading, expands on the theme of baptismal light: 'You were darkness once, but now you are light in the Lord.' The effects of the baptismal light of faith are to be manifested in 'complete goodness, right living and truth.'

When we, like the newly enlightened man of the gospel, believe in Jesus as our Lord, our lives are in constant contact with the source of true light. Faith enables a person to travel through life with expanded vision, seeing with the eyes of God.

He guides me along the right path.

OUT OF THE DEPTHS
Psalm 127

The fifth stage of Old Testament history is the return of the people from exile to the soil of Israel. Ezechiel sees it as God raising them from their graves in a new birth. This first reading harmonises with the raising of Lazarus from the grave, the third baptismal story from John for the catechumens on their journey towards baptism, sacrament of divine life. A prayer for catechumens today reads: 'Lord Jesus, you raised Lazarus from death, as a sign that you had come to give people life in fullest measure.' In today's second reading, Paul contrasts those who are spiritually dead because of sin with those who are newly alive in Christ.

The psalm chosen to give a prayerful response to these readings is the cry from the depths, *De Profundis*. We are so familiar with this as a prayer for the dead that we may not realise that it was originally a cry from the heart of one who was crying *out of the depths* of guilt.

The psalmist prays: *My soul is waiting for the Lord, my soul is longing for the Lord.* But we could equally say that the Lord is waiting for us, longing for us. He awaits the return of the sinner, to lay down the burden of guilt, *because with the Lord there is mercy and fullness of redemption.*

No Lent is complete without an honest examination of life, a humble confession and the joyful celebration of the Lord's mercy.

Out of the depths I cry to you, O Lord.

BEHOLD THE MAN
Psalm 21:8-9, 17-20, 23-24. R/ v 2

They have pierced my hands and feet, they have numbered all my bones.

These words always remind me of the *En Ego*, a favourite prayer of my schoolmaster father, which we recited daily at the end of class. This vivid picture of the suffering Saviour was printed on my young imagination.

These were the hands which welcomed the children and blessed them. Hands whose touch cleansed the leper, opened the eyes of the blind and raised the dead. Hands that welcomed the sinner and broke bread with the outcast. Praying hands raised in adoration or joined in earnest pleading. Expressive hands adding pictures to the words of the preacher.

These were the feet beautiful with the good news brought from village to village. Feet directed in resolute pilgrimage towards Jerusalem.

Good hands and beautiful feet, now pierced with searing metal by sin's mad rejection of the light. Pinioned and closed in a futile attempt to ease the pain.

The psalm we pray today anticipated scenes from the passion of Christ. Jesus cried out, *My God, my God, why have you forsaken me?* Picture all who mock him as *they curl their lips, they toss their heads*. Like dogs they surround him, baying for blood. His clothes are divided and there is a lottery for the seamless robe.

Yet the psalm is a prayer of confidence, leading unto praise. *O Lord, do not leave me alone, my strength, make haste to help me.* The awful scenes of the passion only serve as a dark backdrop to the awesome power of God in the resurrection.

RAISED UP
Psalm 117: 1-2, 16-17, 22-23

This was the last of the *Hallel* psalms which Jesus would have sung with the disciples at the end of the Passover meal. In the light of the resurrection it acquires a wonderful fulfilment. *His right hand has raised me up.* The resurrection completes the passing of Jesus from this world to the Father.

This day was made by the Lord, we rejoice and are glad.

At the great Vigil we celebrated that 'night truly blessed when heaven is wedded to earth'. Ten times the voice of the Cantor proclaimed the significance of that night when darkness was conquered. Day dawns and the women go to the tomb. Lo, the stone is rolled back and the tomb is empty! It is the dawn of a new day ... a day which reaches into eternity.

With the psalmist we rejoice and give thanks for his goodness which has overcome sin, and for his love which has no end. *I shall live and recount his deeds.* We are called to be witnesses to the resurrection, rising above darkness and sin. The most authentic witness is the testimony of charity in thought, attitude and action. God's love comes to perfection only when we love one another. That is how his love has no end.

May the stones of hard hearts be rolled away by the angels of God's grace. May our lives show to the world that he is risen. May the church in its holiness be *a marvel in our eyes.*

BEYOND THE WOUNDS
Psalm 117:2-4, 13-15, 22-24. R/ v 1

Easter joy breaks through the walls of doubt and the light of new day dissolves the shadows of fear. Three times in the psalm we sing aloud that his love has no end. And we give thanks.

Give thanks to the Lord for he is good, for his love has no end.

But there may have been times when we imagined we had gone beyond the scope of God's love. At least, that is how it felt. It seemed to many after Calvary that evil had silenced the good news, that hatred had choked the life out of love, and that death had claimed the ultimate prize. Perhaps we have experienced similar moments of Calvary darkness and feelings of rejection. Like the psalmist, we felt thrust down, falling, drowning in the darkness of guilt and failure. We were stung by harsh words, lack of affirmation or broken promises. Undervalued and rejected. Beyond comfort. Fatigued and dry. Despondent. Like Thomas we found ourselves refusing to believe any good news that others had. We could not see beyond the wounds ... the wounds of our own feelings ... the wounds of the church ... the wounds of others.

But *his love has no end*. God always triumphs. The resurrection is the greatest proof. The breathing of the Spirit announces the grace of forgiveness.

It is resurrection time, time to move on, a season of the Spirit, of grace and of rising.

This day was made by the Lord; we rejoice and are glad.

AN EMMAUS WALK
Psalm 15:1-2, 5, 7-11

In today's reading from the Acts the preaching of Peter applied this psalm to the resurrection .

For you will not leave my soul among the dead,
nor let your beloved know decay.

Easter celebrates a past event ... the Lord has risen. And it also celebrates a present reality ... the Lord is risen. Today's gospel of the disciples on their Emmaus walk exemplifies how the Risen Lord is on the road with us, even when something prevents us from recognising him. Their story begins with the numbing news of what happened in Jerusalem the previous Friday. They have turned their backs on Jerusalem, their faces are downcast and they confess that they have lost hope.

What did the Lord do? He drew their minds back to the scriptures. 'Was it not written?' This is *Lectio Divina* in practice: scripture enabling them to understand the events of life and life's events helping them to understand the scriptures. The event of the previous Friday has not changed but their understanding of it has.

I keep the Lord ever in my sight:
since he is at my right hand, I shall stand firm.

Many distractions and obstacles prevent us from recognising the Risen One on our road. Daily pondering on the scriptures keeps the Lord ever in our sight. We see with new light: our hearts beat with new joy.

You will show me the path of life,
the fullness of joy in your presence,
at your right hand happiness for ever.

SHEPHERDS FOR THE FLOCK
Psalm 22:1-6

The Risen Lord continues to call people to serve in the mission of the church. This Sunday each year is designated as a day of special prayer for vocations: that the church may not lack people who follow the call of the Lord to dedicate their lives in his service.

Jesus takes the image of the shepherd to portray the intimacy of his relationship with those who respond to his call. One by one he calls them. 'I know my own and my own know me.' This God is no stranger but one whose voice is known.

The psalm develops various aspects of this intimate relationship.

The Lord is my Shepherd ... the one whose call is heard and followed.

His presence is the foundation of total trust ... *there is nothing I shall want.*

In times of fatigue *he will give me repose.*

In times of storm *he leads to restful waters.*

His word *guides me along the right path.*

In *the valley of darkness* he casts out fear. It is a source of comfort and strength to know that *you are there.*

You have prepared a banquet for me ... through the ministry of priests, *anointed with oil,* the banquet of the Lord is celebrated.

On Vocations Sunday this is a great prayer of trust that the voice of the Lord will call people to dedicate their lives, *to live in the house of the Lord all the days of my life.*

RESCUED FROM DEATH
Psalm 32:1-2, 4-5, 18-19. R/ v 22

In today's second reading Peter says that Christians are set apart to sing the praises of God. The psalm of the Mass is an invitation to *ring out your joy to the Lord*, to give praise and thanks to God with music and song. This psalm was composed as a hymn to celebrate deliverance from famine and death. The Lord has looked down on the people *to rescue their souls from death, to keep them alive in famine.* The last verse of the psalm, used as the response today, is one of those gems of prayer to be found in the psalms. It is one of my favourite prayers.

May your love be upon us, O Lord,
as we place all our hope in you.

The gospel of the day is the beginning of the section of John's gospel where Jesus gives motives for hope to the disciples when they were troubled by his talk of leaving them. In John, the death of Jesus is not so much his passion as his passing into risen life with the Father. He is going to prepare a place for them, *to rescue their souls from death.*

As Easter advances, the liturgy is beginning to direct our thoughts towards the Ascension of the Lord and the sending of the Holy Spirit. From our fears, troubles and doubts we raise our eyes towards God. Then we are assured that the Spirit of love hovers over us to draw life out of the chaos.

May your love be upon us, O Lord,
as we place all our hope in you.

ENTHUSIASM
Psalm 65:1-7, 16, 20

Enthusiasm is a word that comes from the Greek words for in-God or God-within. The word originally referred to the excited energy of those who really believe in the divine indwelling, the message of today's gospel ... 'I am in my Father and you in me and I in you.'

The psalmist was enthusiastic about an answer he received to prayer for God's protection. He calls on all the earth to cry out with joy to the Lord and to glorify his name. He invites all people to come and *see the works of God, tremendous his deeds among men*. His experience of God's protection was like the passing of the Exodus people through the river dry-shod. The people led out by Moses responded to God's covenant by living in accordance with the commandments carved on tablets of stone. But these laws were disobeyed and the covenant was broken. The new covenant brought by Jesus went beyond laws and was based on responding to God in the inner honesty of love. 'If you love me you will keep my commandments.' Tablets of stone were replaced by hearts of love as the basis for the commandments.

If the psalmist had reason to cry out with joy to the Lord, how much more ought we to be enthusiastic in celebrating the intimacy of divine indwelling. In the second reading Peter tells us 'Reverence the Lord Jesus in your hearts.'

Come and hear, all who fear God.
I will tell what he did for my soul.

THE LORD GOES UP
Psalm 46:2-3, 6-9

All people clap your hands,
cry to God with shouts of joy.

Television shows us massed football fans clapping hands, waving flags and chanting slogans in extraordinary unison. They seem to think and act with one mind.

The psalm's occasion for clapping is, of course, more solemn. It was originally composed for a procession with the Ark of the Covenant. The Ark contained precious memorabilia of the Exodus and of God's covenant with the people. Every year their journey to freedom was celebrated in a great procession with the Ark, up the hill, to the temple. King David was known to have danced with joy on one such occasion, much to the horror of his daughter! Entry into the temple represented their entry into the promised land.

This psalm has acquired a new meaning when applied to the ascension of the Lord. The old covenant has been replaced by Jesus who raises us up in baptism to the dignity of being children of God and heirs of the kingdom of heaven. The Lord Jesus goes up to heaven and where he, the head of the church, has gone, we hope to follow. Heaven itself is now the promised land.

Clap your hands, dance with David, blow the trumpet and sing shouts of joy. We will do it in the sports stadium or concert hall. But why have we become so subdued and reticent in expressing our religious emotion?

Sing praise for God, sing praise,
sing praise with all your skill.

WAITING IN CONFIDENCE
Psalm 26:1, 4, 7-8. R/ v 13

It is the original novena, nine days of waiting in prayer between the Ascension of the Lord and the promised coming of the Holy Spirit. The psalm for the day is a prayer of waiting in total confidence for the Lord's intervention. The response might well have been the prayer of the disciples in their days of waiting:

I am sure I shall see the Lord's goodness
in the land of the living.

I am sure ... how could they be so sure? Where can we draw confidence in times of darkness? They were sure because the Lord had promised the Holy Spirit, comforter, teacher, source of power from on high. We are heirs to the same promises.

I shall see the Lord's goodness in the land of the living. A Spirit-filled life does not wait in dull resignation for 'pie in the sky when we die'. God's goodness is seen on this side of the grave. Peter, in the second reading, sees blessing and gladness in sharing in the sufferings of Christ.

There is one thing that the psalmist asks for with longing. In fact, his request is threefold. It is our prayer too.

May we *live in the house of the Lord*, in union with God's will, all our days.

May we have the grace of savouring *the sweetness of the Lord* ... that prayer will be a such a joy that it gets priority every day.

May we *behold his temple* ... seeing the presence of God in people and situations every day.

Come, Holy Spirit, renew the hearts of the faithful.

THE SPIRIT OF LIFE
Psalm 103:1, 24, 29-31, 34

The writers of the Old Testament attributed the secret of life to the breath or spirit of God. According to the simple cosmology of Genesis, all was emptiness and darkness until the spirit of God breathed over the waters of chaos. This poetic imagery offers more meaning to life than a haphazard big bang theory can do. In the famous vision which Ezechiel had of the valley of dry bones, there was no life in these clattering skeletons until the breath entered them. The writer of today's psalm, a beautiful hymn of creation, expresses this simple belief that life is the gift of God's breath on loan for a while. *You send forth your spirit, they are created.* Then, when the term of mortal life is complete, the breath of life is returned to God.

You take back your spirit, they die,

returning to the dust from which they came.

John's gospel describes Jesus at the last moment of his mortal life giving up his spirit as he breathed his last. His mission in the flesh was accomplished. But then, on the evening of the first day of the risen life, appearing to the disciples he announced the start of the second mission: 'As the Father sent me, so am I sending you'. The mission of the church would be in the same power of the Spirit who had descended on Jesus at the Jordan. So, he breathed on the disciples and said to them: 'Receive the Holy Spirit.'

Come, Holy Spirit, and renew the face of the earth.

GLORY AND PRAISE
Dan 3:52-56

In today's first reading, Moses bowed down to the ground to worship God. The theme of worship is developed in the responsorial psalm, which is taken from the opening verses of the great canticle of creation in the Book of Daniel. Saved from the fiery furnace, the three young men call on all creatures to join them in rendering glory to God. *To you glory and praise for evermore.*

Liberation from that great fire anticipated the great saving deeds of Jesus. The story of the three in the fiery furnace suggests nothing less than the burning fire of God's inner life, where the Three Persons are distinct but united in knowledge and love. This love is shown in Jesus. As Jesus said to Nicodemus: 'God loved the world so much that he gave his only Son, so that everyone who believes in him may not be lost but may have eternal life.'

Daniel called on all creatures to join him in prayer. We have the higher privilege, granted through baptism, of participating in the very hymns of heaven. When the love of the Father sent the Son to earth, the perfect praise that was sung in heaven came into our world. In his return to the Father, we too are lifted up to share in the perfect praise. It is our privilege in sacred liturgy to render all honour and glory to the Father, through Jesus, with him and in him, by the sanctifying power of the Holy Spirit.

To you glory and praise for evermore.

BREAD FROM HEAVEN
Psalm 147:12-15, 19-20

The church, here called Jerusalem, praises God for the blessings
of being a chosen and favoured people. The focus of today's
feast is on the Blessed Eucharist, the gift of Christ's sacred Body
and Blood.

He feeds you with finest wheat. The psalm follows the words of
Moses reminding the chosen people how they were fed during
the Exodus journey with the gift of manna from heaven. It was
called the food of angels, containing every delight, satisfying
every taste and transformed into what each eater wished
(Wisdom 16:21). It foreshadowed the Eucharist.

He sends out his word to the earth and swiftly runs his command.
In the fullness of time God sent his Word to become flesh in the
womb of Mary. Then at the last supper, the word of Jesus was a
divine command which changed the bread and wine into his
own loving presence to sustain us on the pilgrimage of life ...
'my flesh to eat, my blood to drink.' Belief in the presence of the
Lord in the consecrated bread and wine is based on the words of
Jesus. If the physical body of Jesus had been subjected to scientific testing there would have been no evidence of his divinity.
Similarly, scientific testing of the Eucharist would not show the
presence of the Lord. It is a matter of belief, belief founded on
the word of the Lord.

He has not dealt thus with other nations ... no other people have
such a divine gift.

O praise the Lord, Jerusalem.

TO DO YOUR WILL
Psalm 39:2, 4, 7-10

The psalmist has received God's favour after long waiting. Now he must respond to God. Will it be in the sacrifice of animals? He admits that the external ritual of sacrifice is empty without the inner dispositions of total obedience to God's law.

You do not ask for holocaust and victim.
Instead, here am I.
In the scroll of the book it stands written
that I should do your will.

The Letter to the Hebrews applies these words to Jesus at his coming into the world. Like the psalmist who *waited and waited for the Lord*, the people had longed for the coming of the Messiah. In Jesus, the Lord *stooped down* to the human level. In his total obedience to the Father he laid down his life in sacrifice. In today's gospel Jesus is identified by John the Baptist as the lamb of God. He is the lamb of sacrifice who not only atoned for sin, but he took away the sins of the world. Sacrifice and obedience are perfectly united in Jesus. All previous sorts of animal substitutes have been rendered redundant.

The image of the lamb also recalled the picture of the meek and obedient lamb being led to the slaughter. The perfect yes of Jesus to the Father in all things is an inspiration to us to seek the will of God in all that we do.

Here I am Lord!
I come to do your will.

LIGHT AND HOPE
Psalm 26:1, 4, 13-14

As the gospel of the day opens up the public ministry of Jesus, our psalm is a beautiful prayer of trust. *The Lord is my light and my help*. The theme of light links up with the words of Isaiah, repeated in the gospel: 'The people that walked in darkness has seen a great light.' When Jesus began to preach, the light of God's revelation shone into the darkness of soul and mind. 'On those who dwell in the land and shadow of death a light has dawned.' Jesus is the light that vanquishes spiritual, moral and emotional darkness. He is light to the spirit in his life-giving word. Moral light in showing us how to live. And the news of God's love which he brings is the light which banishes the clouds of fear and depression.

The Lord is my light and my help;
whom shall I fear?

There is one thing that the psalmist longs for ... a lasting experience of the presence of the Lord all his days. The first disciples were drawn by the call of Jesus to leave family and work to follow him. The temple of his presence is no longer a building of stones but every part of life illuminated by faith. Yet faith is but a dim anticipation of the full beatific vision. Our hope is that we shall one day see the Lord's goodness in the land of eternal life. In his light, we travel forward in hope.

Hope in him, hold firm and take heart.
Hope in the Lord.

BLESSED ARE THE POOR
Psalm 145:7-10

What is sometimes called the Prosperity Gospel or Cadillac Christianity, advocated by many tele-evangelists, is built on a simplistic idea of God's blessing. They say that health, success and prosperity are certain signs of God's blessing on a good life. But what about those who are suffering misfortune? Their answer is that misfortune is a sure sign that the afflicted one is a sinner who is being punished by God. Or it may be for the sins of a family member, even from a previous generation of the family tree.

Jesus utterly rejected this simplistic notion. He turned upside down the Deuteronomy concept of material blessings as a reward for obeying the law. He proclaimed the blessedness of the poor and powerless, of those who strive for justice and of those who are victims of injustice.

The psalm of the day proclaims that God's love is faithful for ever.

It is he who keeps faith for ever,
who is just to those who are oppressed.

Anticipating the beatitudes of Jesus, the psalmist is confident of God's blessing upon those who are suffering bad fortune at the moment, listing the oppressed, the hungry, prisoners, the blind, those bowed down under heavy burdens, the stranger, widow and orphan.

God's faithful love operates on a long timescale. In the beatitudes, all the promised consolations are in the future tense. But even now, those suffering misfortune are the blessed who belong to God's kingdom.

Blessed are the poor in spirit; theirs is the kingdom of heaven.

BEARERS OF THE LIGHT
Psalm 111:4-9

In the Sermon on the Mount, Jesus follows the beatitudes with the statement to the disciples that they are the salt of the earth and the light of the world. The light of good works is the theme of today's readings. The motto of the Christophers states that it is better to light one candle than to curse the darkness. Christopher means one who carries Christ. The light of Christ is handed on to the newly baptised as a responsibility: 'You are the light of the world.'

Today's psalm celebrates some practical examples of how to carry the light. In relationships with others, we reflect Christ's light in being *generous, merciful and just,* when we *take pity and lend,* and when we conduct our affairs with honour. In relationship with God, darkness is overcome by faith which does not waver and by such depth of trust that we have *no fear of evil news.*

The good man is a light in the darkness for the upright .

Whoever lives with such radiant virtues renders glory to God in a very practical way. It reminds one of the observation of St Irenaeus that the glory of God is seen in the person who is fully alive, whose face is turned towards God.

'Let your light shine in the sight of people, so that seeing your good works, they may give the glory to your Father in heaven.'

THE WONDERS OF THE LAW
Psalm 118:1-2, 4-5, 17-18, 33-34

Open my eyes that I may consider
the wonders of your law.

We do not usually consider law as an area of wonder. Laws are regarded as boundaries we ought not transgress rather than as thresholds of wonder. In Jewish mentality, however, what was called the law was more than a collection of laws or decrees. The whole was greater than the sum of the parts. The law of God meant the revelation of God's will. For the people, the law was the precious statement of God's covenant of love with his chosen people.

In the law would be found God's word, God's wisdom and God's love. Pondering on the law would bring truth and wisdom: promise and trust: light and direction. Today's responsorial psalm is a short selection from the long psalm in which each couplet is a gem of wise and holy reflection on the gift of the law. The law provides a light for my path and a lamp for my steps. It revives the soul and teaches wisdom to the simple. Seeking God's law leads to a blameless life and makes one's footsteps firm.

To a people who held God's law in sacred regard, Jesus announced that he had not come to abolish it but to complete it. In him, the Word made flesh, the revelation of God's loving covenant with us is complete.

Train me to observe your law,
to keep it with my heart.

DIVINE FORGIVENESS
Psalm 102:1-4, 8, 10, 12-13

Today's psalm corrects the popular but mistaken notion that the Old Testament was all about a stern God of strict justice. *The Lord is compassion and love, slow to anger and rich in mercy.* Not only does God have compassion but God *is* compassion. In other words, it is the nature of God to be always compassionate.

In the Sermon on the Mount Jesus sets up the ideal of not returning one wrong for another but of overcoming injustices by the greater power of love. 'In this way you will be children of your Father in heaven.' Children inherit the features of the parents.

There are different stages in responding to a wrong that has been suffered. At the lowest level, the hurt cries out for revenge and personal retaliation. One step higher is to let the due process of law establish the terms of retribution. In this case justice is sought in equitable compensation or in the form of a punishment to fit the crime. While justice seeks to restore the moral order of right and wrong, there may still be a deep residue of hurt feelings. What is needed is forgiveness, a Godlike attribute which can heal the inner hurt and restore the broken relationship.

Our psalm today invites us to thank God for the blessings of divine forgiveness for *all your guilt ... every one of your ills ... who crowns you with love and compassion. He does not treat us according to our sins, nor repay us for all our faults.* The challenge is to be perfect just as your heavenly Father is perfect.

AT HOME, AT REST
Psalm 61:1-3, 6-9

It has been said that a person can survive for eight minutes without air, for forty days without food but not for one moment without hope. Today's readings are about the inner security to be drawn from resting our hopes in God alone. Isaiah invokes a maternal image, attributing to God the qualities of a mother's memory. 'Does a woman forget her baby at the breast, or fail to cherish the son of her womb?' Just as the mother of Jesus 'treasured all these things in her heart', a mother's memory is a bond of life that cannot be broken. Turning to today's gospel we have the paternal image of God as the heavenly Father who provides for the birds of the air and the flowers of the field.

The verses of the psalm chosen to link these readings express profound trust and great inner security. *In God alone is my soul at rest.* God is *my rock, my stronghold, my fortress, my safety and my glory.* The repetition of the possessive pronoun *my* confirms the depth of the psalmist's personal relationship with God. Memory, collective and personal, is the strongest factor in coming to know our identity. The psalmist knows who he is in relation to God and so he can say that in God alone is his soul at rest.

What does it mean to be at rest? It suggests coming home, and home, as I heard a wise man say, is where you lay your bones at the end of the day. *In God alone be my soul at rest.*

AN EVERLASTING ROCK
Psalm 30:2-4, 17, 25. R/ v 3

This psalm is a prayer of immense confidence, at a time of distress and shame, anticipating God's favourable intervention.

Let your face shine on your servant.

Save me in your love.

The image of *the rock of refuge* connects with the Lord's parable at the end of the Sermon on the Mount.

The psalmist thinks of the rock as a shelter from enemies, a place of *refuge*, a *stronghold*, a site easy to defend. It calls to mind the old cowboy films, with a rocky outcrop offering shelter from whirring arrows and whistling bullets.

In the Lord's sermon, the rock is an image of solid foundation, in contrast to the sandy foundation which is worthless. Those who listen to the word of the Lord and put it into practice are building the house of life on a solid foundation.

The sandy foundation under a shaky house is an apt image of the restless agitation which afflicts many today. A major cause of stress is trying to cope with the rapid pace of change. Just when I knew the answers, they changed the questions! More access to information, easier travel and the startling possibilities of technology have bred the desire to test and taste everything. Trouble is that loyalty, fidelity and commitment suffer. The umbrella of pluralism shelters a reprehensible tolerance of behaviour which contradicts the commandments ... a cursed state, in today's first reading.

The teaching of Jesus is an everlasting rock, offering

- truth that never changes;
- hope that never fades;
- and love that never grows old.

THE VALUE OF SACRIFICE
Psalm 49:1, 8, 12-15

The readings in today's liturgy are about offering sacrifices to God. In the psalm, God assures the people of the merit of their offerings:

> *I find no fault with your sacrifices,*
> *your offerings are always before me.*
> *Pay your sacrifice of thanksgiving to God*
> *and render him your votive offerings.*

However, the first reading and the gospel of the day make the point that religious rituals are empty if they are not backed up by love and mercy. What God wants is mercy or love rather than empty sacrifice.

The fact is that God has no need of any kind of sacrifice. The need is on our side. We need every aid available to help us focus our distracted lives on our relationship with God. Personal acts of sacrifice can help us in a variety of ways, such as enabling us to show our appreciation of God's gifts in thanksgiving, or acknowledging the majesty of God in adoration or in showing the sincerity of our sorrow for sin. If we back up our words of petition with personal sacrifices it adds authenticity to our prayer. In common parlance, we put our money where our mouth is ... which is precisely what Matthew did in leaving his toll booth to follow Jesus. But when all is said and done, it is the inner conversion of heart which gives merit to the outward action. One act of mercy or practical charity pleases God more than a thousand words. As the Lord said: 'What I want is mercy, not sacrifice.'

ON EAGLE'S WINGS
Psalm 99:2-3, 5

One of the loveliest images of God's love occurs in today's First Reading: 'I carried you on eagle's wings and brought you to my-self.' The eagle builds its nest on a ledge in a high cliff. When the time comes for the young eaglet to venture to the air for the first time, the mother, flying out, encourages the young one to fol-low. When the young wings tire, the mother swoops underneath to carry the offspring to safety.

The gospel transfers the imagery of caring to the world of the shepherd. Jesus felt sorry for the people, harassed and dejected, like sheep without a shepherd. He commissioned the twelve apostles and gave them his message and divine power. The church, founded on the apostles, continues God's work of caring and carrying, of teaching and feeding.

In today's second reading Paul writes that what proves that God loves us is the way that Christ died for us while we were sinners. On the cross, Jesus was the one who carried our sins and bore our sufferings.

One function of the responsorial psalm is to give us the lang-uage of prayer to respond to the readings. Today's psalm tells us to *know that he, the Lord, is God: he made us, we belong to him, we are his people, the sheep of his flock*. Our God, we are told, is *good, full of merciful and faithful*. We are encouraged to sing for joy and to offer a service that is characterised by gladness.

TAUNTED BUT UNBROKEN
Psalm 68:8-10, 14, 17, 33-35

These verses are taken from one of the great psalms of lamentation. In our first verse we are given some idea of the burden of
opposition faced by the psalmist. He is subjected to so much
taunting that he feels that his face is clothed with shame. He is a
stranger to his brothers, an alien to his own mother's sons. And
why? All because of his zeal for the house of God. We recall that
Jesus quoted these very words when he drove the money-
changers out of the temple.

In the first reading Jeremiah recounts the taunts thrown at
him. And in the gospel Jesus prepares the apostles for a hostile
reception. Three times he repeats the words, 'Do not be afraid.'

The situation has not changed. Just as light hurts the sore eye,
so will godliness stir up hatred in the sick soul. People who
stand up for Christian principles are frequently subjected to bul-
lying, emotional pressure or mockery. They are taunted with in-
sulting names ... fundamentalist, conservative, right-winger, out
of date!

The psalmist, in the second verse, rises up from his wounded
feelings to fervent prayer. *In your great love, answer me, O God,
with your help that never fails.*

So confident is he of God's favourable answer that, in the
third verse, his prayer anticipates a favourable answer and advances into praise of God. The saintly American Capuchin,
Solanus Casey, would tell people that since God already knew
their petitions, they should spend fewer words in petition and
thank God ahead of time.

*The Lord listens to the needy
and does not spurn his servants in their chains.*

FAITHFUL AND STEADFAST
Psalm 88:2-3, 16-19

When Jesus sent out the apostles, he emphasised that the privilege of serving the good news demands a full commitment of mind and heart, even to the extent of placing the call of God's word above family. The support that one would normally draw from immediate family would be transcended by the welcome offered by those who receive and appreciate the good news. The first reading recalls the woman of Shunem who resolved to offer hospitality to Elisha because he was a bearer of the word.

The three psalm verses chosen to accompany these readings are taken from a very long psalm of lament and hope. The context of the psalm is a lament for the calamities happening to Jerusalem, but the psalmist finds hope when he remembers the promises made to David. Because God's word is faithful, he confidently looks forward to the time of the messianic king. The verses we use today express this hope:

Of this I am sure, that your love lasts for ever,
through all ages my mouth will proclaim your truth,
that your truth is firmly established as the heavens.

The psalm then proclaims the happiness of those who *walk in the light of your face, who find their joy every day in your name, who make your justice the source of their bliss.*

But there are times when answering the call of the Lord is not easy. At such difficult times, like the psalmist, we draw hope from recalling the fidelity of the Lord's promise.

I will sing forever of your love, O Lord.

COME TO ME
Psalm 144

If one is to judge by the books that top the bestseller lists, stories of unhappy childhoods in dysfunctional families exercise a morbid fascination for people. The gospel however reflects a golden childhood in which wisdom is imparted through care and trust. 'I bless you, Father, Lord of heaven and earth, for hiding these things from the learned and clever and revealing them to mere children.' Just as Jesus blessed the Father, today's psalm invites us to return praise for the kindness and compassion of God.

Ponder prayerfully on these qualities of God. *The Lord is kind ... full of compassion ... slow to anger ... abounding in love ... good to all ... compassionate to all his creatures ... faithful in all his words ... loving in all his deeds.* Notice the universality of God's embrace as expressed in the recurring use of the word *all*.

Anybody who claims that the Old Testament is all about a stern, judgemental God must have never read this psalm or similar passages. In today's passage from the Old Testament, Zechariah looks forward to the reign of the king of peace, riding on a donkey, associated with service, rather than on a horse, associated with war. The invitation of Jesus goes out to all who are burdened to come to him and he will give them rest. *The Lord supports all who fall and raises all who are bowed down.*

I will bless your name for ever,
O God, my King.

IN PRAISE OF RAIN
Psalm 64:10-14

A psalm in praise of rain! It echoes the words of Isaiah about the rain and the snow coming down from the heavens to make the earth fertile, an image of how the word of God gives growth to our spiritual lives. The gospel of the sower illustrates the need for the soil to be ready to receive the dynamic potential of the seed. The seed is the word of God and the soil is the earthy texture of our thoughts, attitudes and behaviour. Rain softens the hard ground and the grace of God softens the hard heart.

Is it tempting providence to sing in praise of rain around the time of Saint Swithin's feast? In the lush land of Ireland we pray more often for the cessation of rain than for its pouring. Especially at holiday time.

Your river in heaven brims over ... hardly a scientific explanation but what a fascinating picture! Our psalm lists the providential acts of God. *You care for the earth, give it water, you fill it, you provide, you drench, you level, you soften, you bless, you crown the year with your goodness.*

We would not have our forty shades of green without our forty varieties of rain. Where would we be without this bounty from the sky? *Hills are girded with joy, meadows covered with flocks and valleys are decked with wheat.* May there be enough rain to satisfy farmer and fisherman but not too much to spoil the holidays. Praise the Lord!

YOU GOVERN US WITH GREAT LENIENCE
Psalm 85:5-6, 9-10, 15-16

This psalm appeals to the compassion and forgiveness of God. Sometimes we may be tempted to ask why doesn't God strike down the tyrant, the war monger, the drug baron or the evil person who makes life a misery for others? We are inclined to forget that these people are God's children too and that the compassion of God offers the hope of repentance to all.

Today's reading from the Book of Wisdom teaches that the God of sovereign power is mild in judgement and governs with great lenience: like that wise farmer in today's gospel parable who does not destroy the wheat by pulling up the darnel. Every opportunity is given to repent and grow before the final sorting out. God's love extends to all his creatures, even to the most evil sinner whose behaviour totally contradicts the image and likeness of God. God's love can never be anything less than 100% since God *is* love.

O Lord, you are good and forgiving
full of love to all who call.

The psalmist makes an earnest plea for a favourable hearing in a time of distress. Notice the clever bargaining. If you are seen to answer our prayers, Lord, all the nations will come to adore you. I'm sure God has the humour to enjoy such cajoling.

God of mercy and compassion,
Slow to anger, O Lord,
abounding in love and truth,
turn and take pity on me.

LORD, HOW I LOVE YOUR LAW
Psalm 118:57, 72, 76-77, 127-130

Solomon prayed for a gift worth more than gold and silver when he asked for the light to discern between good and evil. The guidance of God's law is the treasure hidden in the field, the pearl beyond price. The psalm which links these two readings is the psalmist's declaration of love for the revelation of God's wisdom contained in the law. *Lord, how I love your law!* When the Jews spoke about the law they were referring not just to moral commands and ritual regulations but to the wisdom guiding one's entire response of thought, emotion and behaviour to the God of the covenant.

Psalm 118 is a long psalm rejoicing in the gift of God's law. Each of the twenty-two letters of the Hebrew alphabet is used in turn to begin eight verses of four lines. In each pair of lines we find some synonym for the law of God. In today's verses we hear of God's word ... law ... promise ... commands ... precepts ... will ... word. The psalmist regards the law not as a restricting burden but as the gift of God's wisdom to guide us on our road of life. *That is why I love your commands more than finest gold.*

The Prayer of the Church takes a section of this psalm practically every day at midday to call our wandering ways back to God's law. Every day it asks us whether we are seeking God's will or our own way.

The unfolding of your will gives light
and teaches the simple.

GRACE BEFORE MEAL
Psalm 144:8-9, 15-18

The eyes of all creatures look to you
and you give them their food in due time.
You open wide your hand,
grant the desires of all who live.

The picture is like feeding time at the zoo, mouths open, hands reaching. Indeed this verse has often been used as part of grace before meals. It connects with today's gospel as a prayer before the miraculous feeding of the people with five loaves and two fishes. The Lord who is *kind and full of compassion* took pity on the people and healed the sick. Then he fed them with the wonderfully multiplied loaves and fishes. Nor was there any stinting in his generosity for there were twelve baskets left over, one for each apostle.

But, as they say, there is no such thing as a free dinner, and those who are the recipients of God's bounty are expected to give in turn to others. 'Give them something to eat yourselves.' We who hear his word today and are fed on the bread of his sacred presence will be sent out at the end of Mass to love and serve the Lord.

'This is a lonely place.' Notice how the word *all* occurs no fewer than seven times in our psalm. The miracle of the Lord's bread must not be locked up in the tabernacle. His love is for all. Take up your basket which the Lord has filled and give the food of God's love to others.

A VOICE OF PEACE
Psalm 84:9-14

I will hear what the Lord God has to say. Well that's a change from our more usual prayer when God has to listen to what we have to say! Look at Elijah on the holy mountain anticipating the Lord in thundering majesty. But no, in this instance the divine word came not in the mighty wind, the earthquake or the fire, but in the gentlest of breezes. Silence is the place where God is most easily heard.

A voice that speaks of peace ... his help is near for those who fear him.

Now picture Peter, his boat tossed on the stormy sea. He catches a glimpse of the Lord passing by. As long as he keeps his eye on the Lord he can walk on water. But once he looks at the waves he begins to sink. Then the Lord's hand reaches out to save him. The story of Jesus, watching from on high, and coming to the storm-tossed boat of the disciples, is a source of great hope for the church in these troubled times. Look only at the problems and we sink, but look at Jesus and everything is possible.

Mercy and faithfulness have met;
justice and peace have embraced.

These are intriguing lines. Perhaps they suggest that strict justice on its own would not be sufficient for us, given our propensity to fall again and again. So God showed the faithfulness of his love, and in this embrace that we call mercy, peace is to be found.

Justice shall march before him
and peace shall follow his steps.

THE FACE OF CHRIST
Psalm 66:2-3, 5-6, 8

Let the peoples praise you, O God,
let all the peoples praise you.

The psalmist, like Isaiah in the first reading, looks forward to the time when all nations will share in the spiritual blessings of the Jews. In the gospel, Jesus praises the faith of the Canaanite woman, a foreigner.

One line of the psalm stands out for me. *Let your face shed its light upon us.* The letter of Pope John Paul II for the new millennium might be called a contemplation of the face of Christ. Jesus Christ is the human face of God: a face of wisdom and inspiration: a face of mercy and compassion: the face of solidarity with those who suffer: the face of the Risen Lord radiant with divine glory. We pray for the grace of experiencing a smile of light from the Lord's face, just like the Canaanite woman begging for even a crumb from the table.

A very different sort of face was pictured by Oliver Goldsmith in his portrait of the village schoolmaster.

Well had the boding tremblers learned to trace
The day's disasters in his morning face.

Christians are commissioned at baptism to carry the light of the good news. As Paul put it: 'It is the same God that said "Let there be light shining out of darkness", who has shone in our minds to radiate the light of the knowledge of God's glory, the glory on the face of Christ.' If you believe you are saved pass the message to your face!

KEYS OF AUTHORITY
Psalm 137:1-3, 6, 8

The keys of authority feature in the first reading and in the gospel of the day. The psalm is, first of all, a prayer of gratitude and, then, a prayer of confidence that God's faithful love will not cease to support the one who was chosen. *Your love, O Lord, is eternal, discard not the work of your hands.*

When Jesus bestowed the keys of authority on Simon Peter, he promised that the powers of the underworld would never overcome his church. Pope Benedict XVI, in his earlier writings, pointed out that the word *hierarchy* comes from a Greek word for the origin or beginning of something. The authority of the hierarchy is the responsibility of staying true to our origins, that is, to the teaching of Christ.

I thank you for your faithfulness and love
which excel all we ever knew of you.

Christ's promise is a sure foundation because his love is faithful and his word is eternal. He gave Simon the new name, Peter, a rock, the promise of stability. The house founded on solid rock would withstand any storm.

There have been some sinful popes and at times the papacy has been an obstacle to unity, but these defects are far outweighed by the gift of holy and wise leadership that the good popes have offered. On our lips this psalm becomes a prayer for the church and the successor of Peter.

Your love, O Lord, is eternal,
discard not the work of your hands.

THIRSTING FOR GOD
Psalm 62:2-6, 8-9

O God, you are my God, for you I long;
for you my soul is thirsting.

Has there ever been a more passionate expression of the soul's desire for God? It is a thirst in the inner soul, a pining in the body. Saint Augustine famously wrote of the restless longing which is not satisfied until the soul rests in God. In today's first reading Jeremiah described it as an overpowering seduction, a fire burning in his heart, imprisoned in his bones. Like the missing piece of a jigsaw, there is a God-shaped emptiness in the human heart.

My body pines for you,
like a dry, weary land without water.

Love takes time. The desire for God calls one to spend time gazing in the sanctuary, soaking oneself in God's strength and glory.

So I gaze on you in the sanctuary
to see your strength and your glory.

The gospel asks the eternal question, what does it profit one to win all that the world has to offer but to ruin one's inner life? *Your love is better than life.*

The mouth that we use to chew our food is the same organ which is filled with praise and blessing. *So I will bless you all my life.* No earthly banquet can compare with the heavenly joy of praising the Lord and knowing the warmth of God's loving protection.

In the shadow of your wings I rejoice.
My soul clings to you.
Your right hand holds me fast.

HARDEN NOT YOUR HEARTS
Psalm 94:1-2, 6-9

It is important to remember that the promise of the Lord to be with those who gather in his name was originally spoken in the context of fraternal correction. Correction is the theme of today's readings. Ezechiel says that whoever fails to correct an errant sentry shares responsibility for the abdication of duty.

The psalm chosen to enhance this theme is the great invitation to worship, normally used at the beginning of Morning Prayer. The first verse is the invitation to come and celebrate with joy and thanksgiving the God who saves us. The second verse draws attention to some of the dispositions of mind and body which prepare the soul for true worship: *let us bow and bend low; let us kneel before the God who made us.* Any time you experienced the inner need to genuflect or kneel in adoration, it was a moment to treasure. Our outward, bodily demeanour helps us attain an inner spirit of submission to God.

The psalm then confronts an obstacle to prayer ... hardness of heart. *O that today you would listen to his voice!* The word *listen* occurs four times in the gospel's instruction on offering correction to someone who has gone astray. *Harden not your hearts as at Massah ... and Meribah.* These were places where people grumbled and rebelled against God. Have we allowed our grumbling and cynicism to harden our hearts? Taking correction is not easy but remember that it is the Lord who speaks through those who meet in his name to offer us correction.

Listen to his voice ... harden not your hearts.

FORGIVENESS
Psalm 102:1-4, 9-12

The first reading and gospel today are about forgiving others while the psalm praises God for his compassion and mercy. *The Lord is compassion and love, slow to anger and rich in mercy.*

The gospel begins with Peter asking Jesus how often he must forgive his brother if he wrongs him. Brothers don't always have the happiest of relationships in the Old Testament. Think of Cain and Abel, Isaac and Ishmael, Jacob and Esau, Joseph and his jealous brothers. Most of the trouble in our lives comes from those who are nearest to us.

In Jesus Christ we see the triumph of goodness over evil, and of mercy over sin. The instinct of fallen nature after an offence is towards resentment and anger ... foul things, according to Ecclesiasticus. The parable in today's gospel makes the point that the forgiveness we receive from God is something we must pass on to others.

The Catechism of the Catholic Church teaches that the outpouring of God's mercy cannot penetrate our hearts as long as we have not forgiven those who have trespassed against us. People are encouraged to visit the memory of past hurts. But staying in the past brings no healing. Constant picking at the scars reverses the healing process. With the grace of the Holy Spirit we can reach a higher plane where the wrongs of others are seen in a different light.

As the heavens are high above the earth
so strong is his love for those who fear him.
As far as the east is from the west
so far does he remove our sins.

CLOSE TO ALL
Psalm 144:2-3, 8-9, 17-18

Today's psalm recognises many qualities of God: greatness beyond measure, kindness, compassion and love in abundance. Above all, it rejoices that God is always near. *The Lord is close to all who call him.* A message on a flipchart in a retreat centre appealed to me: *If you think you are a million miles from God, guess who moved?*

We might think that sin has set us far distant from God. But God's thoughts are not our thoughts. The point of today's parable is that God's generosity goes far beyond the limits of strict justice. Notice how the word *all* keeps recurring in the psalm. God is *good to all, compassionate to all. God is just in all his ways and loving in all his deeds. He is close to all who call on him from their hearts.* As Saint John wrote, God is love, and so God's love is never less than 100%. It excludes nobody.

The mobile phone has made communication with friends very easy. Easier still is communication with God for those who have given over their hearts in the act of faith. The Lord is close to us. The question remains, am I close to God? Close in thought, in attitude and behaviour. God loves me 365 days of the year. Prayer must be my response to God 365 days of the year. Guess who moved!

I will bless you day after day and praise your name for ever.

THE MIND OF CHRIST
Psalm 24:4-9

At the recent publication of the revised *Oxford English Dictionary* it was pointed out that there are ten expressions of a negative state of mind for every one expression of a positive state. In today's second reading we are exhorted to change our minds into the thinking of Jesus Christ. Jesus gave such positive hope to the sinner and the outcast that he shocked the people who regarded themselves as being on the right side. Ezechiel also dealt with people who were scandalised by God's forgiveness.

The psalm of the day is an appeal to the mercy of God. I am particularly taken by the lines:

Do not remember the sins of my youth.
In your love remember me
because of your goodness, O Lord.

Many people are haunted by guilt over their misdemeanours of years ago. They focus so much on the negative that they do not sufficiently appreciate the merciful love of God. To repeat what is already said, Jesus shocked people with the positive hope he gave to the sinner. In the wisdom of the church we do not merely confess our sins privately to God, but we are asked to come to a sacrament to celebrate reconciliation. All sacraments are celebrations of the grace-filled presence of the Risen Lord.

If we ask God to remember us in love, we must be prepared to let go of our negative memories of what others have done to us. To enter the mind of Christ we pray:

Lord, make me know your ways.
Lord, teach me your paths.

VISIT THIS VINE
Psalm 79:9, 12-16, 19-20

The vineyard is an image of God's chosen people, led out of slavery in Egypt and planted in a land of their own. But an unfaithful people were in danger of losing their inheritance to foreign invaders. *Visit this vine and protect it, the vine your right hand has planted.*

Praying this psalm about the vineyard under assault, my thoughts are for the church which is experiencing a winter season here in Western Europe. I grew up in a church proud of its great calling and holy saints: very fruitful in vocations and spreading its branches in vigorous mission. How things have changed! Our walls of confidence are broken down, we are ravaged by scandals and devoured by hostile critics. Our age profile is alarmingly high and our missionary energy is bled dry. Yet we believe it is God's church, planted by his hand and nourished by his grace. So, we call on God to visit us once more, to protect and renew us. On our part we repent of our sins and promise that *we will never forsake you again.*

At the edge of the abyss, the only way forward is to go back ... back to where we started. The way forward is in contemplation of Jesus Christ, the human face of God. As Pope John Paul II wrote: 'No, we shall not be saved by a formula but by a person. and the assurance which he gives us: I am with you.'

With the psalmist we pray:

Let your face shine on us and we shall be saved.

INVITATION TO THE BANQUET
Psalm 22

Today's liturgy celebrates the Lord's gracious invitation to come to his banquet. Isaiah proclaimed a banquet of rich food and fine wines. God's invitation to us is reflected in the way that the shepherd goes before the sheep, inviting them to follow. He leads me ... he guides me ... he protects me in the valley of darkness and he invites me to his banquet all prepared. According to a local shepherd's interpretation, the foes of the sheep are all the harmful weeds which have been cleared beforehand by the shepherd. Sheep can safely graze in the sight of these noxious bundles.

For Christians, the banquet of the Lord refers especially to the Eucharist. Jesus has become our Bread of Life. As the manna was God's bread to support the people through the exodus, the Eucharist is the divine food which strengthens us against our foes and temptations.

The Lord has prepared the banquet. He sends out the invitations. But, as in the parable of today, many do not take up the invitation. There is one startling observation ... 'they were not interested.' One was more interested in his farm, another in his business and so on. Today we can add sport, Sunday shopping, holidays and morning-after hangovers to the list. Spiritual apathy.

You have prepared a banquet for me in the sight of my foes. Though we know that we are not worthy, yet blessed are those who hear his word and are called to his supper.

In the Lord's own house shall I dwell
for ever and ever.

RENDER TO GOD
Psalm 95:1, 3-5, 7-10

Today's readings mention two of the greatest leaders of ancient times, Cyrus of Persia and Caesar of Rome, powerful leaders with military authority, acting like gods in their empires, yet subject to the eternal majesty of God. 'Render to Caesar what belongs to Caesar, but to God what belongs to God.'

The psalm of the day is an invitation to pay joyful homage to God, above all others, the maker of heaven and earth.

The Lord is great and worthy of praise,
to be feared above all gods;
the gods of the heathens are naught.
It was the Lord who made the heavens.

The false gods worshipped today are associated with wealth, celebrity status or popular fashion ... *the gods of the heathens* ... but they are incapable of satisfying the deep needs of our spirit. There is one God, the beginning and the end of all, who alone is to be adored and worshipped. *Bring an offering and enter his courts.* The offering of the Eucharist is the perfect praise of God.

The psalmist wants the glory of God to be celebrated by the people of every nation. The Christian story is wonderful news which the whole world has the right to hear. It is news which offers meaning, hope and transcendence to human life. It is a story that never grows old. Each morning it calls for a new song to the Lord.

Tell among the nations his glory
and his wonders among all the peoples.

I LOVE YOU, LORD MY STRENGTH
Psalm 17:2-4, 47, 50

This psalm is attributed to King David as a prayer of gratitude to God who has been his protector in countless battles and dangers. The images have all the hardness of the military world ... *my strength, my rock, my fortress, my saviour, my shield, my mighty help, my stronghold ... the rock where I take refuge.*

The mood of David's response to God is a mixture of macho glorification and tenderness. He sounds like a victorious captain holding aloft the spoils of victory, proclaiming: *Long life to the Lord, my rock!* Yet there is a quieter, more tender side which says: *I love you, Lord, my strength.* He recognises that the protection he has enjoyed comes from God's love.

He has given great victories to his king
and shown his love for his anointed.

David has the fundamental disposition of true religion, namely an appreciation of the love of God. He is moved to recount God's favours, to lift up his voice in praise and, above all, to love God with all his heart and soul and mind. The point made in today's gospel is that the primary function of religious laws and teaching is to show us how to love God and neighbour. Perhaps David sees that the power and authority given to him by God were to be used in justice and concern for the poor. The first reading spells out several practical ways of loving one's neighbour.

I love you, Lord, my strength
my rock, my fortress, my saviour.

DOWN TO EARTH HUMILITY
Psalm 130

It is not often that we get a complete psalm at Mass. This short psalm is really a little gem. It is the prayer of those who know their place before God. This attitude before God results in the twin virtues of humility and trustfulness.

Humility is a word that comes from the Latin, *humus,* meaning the earth. Humility means down-to-earth truthfulness about yourself ... about others ... and about God. It recognises one's talents as well as one's limitations.

I have not gone after things too great
nor marvels beyond me.

The Italian novelist, Manzoni, described people who are full of humility when it comes to placing themselves beneath others but not when it is a matter of being their equals. You know the sort ... stubbornly proud of their humility! Bogus humility has given the virtue a suspect name.

The opposite of humility is pride, which brings out ugly traits in the personality. It makes people haughty, judgemental and competitive ... like the Pharisees in today's gospel. Pride makes people think they have no need of God. But the humble soul is happy to recognise our need of God. This gives one access to a supernatural source of help. Trustfulness is a fruit of humility. Like the contented child reposing in mother's arms, the soul finds strength and serenity in God.

Constant repetition of this little psalm can be a source of peace and serenity.

O Lord, my heart is not proud,
nor haughty my eyes.

THIRSTING FOR GOD
Psalm 62:2-8

November calls us to attend to our final destiny. The parable of the bridesmaids is a lesson on being spiritually alert to the coming of the Lord. The psalm is the prayer of one whose life is totally centred on God, day and night. Every part of the psalmist's life is reaching towards God like a flower towards the sun. His heart is longing for God, his soul is thirsting and his body is pining, *like a dry, weary land without water.*

Prayer blossoms in many ways. Sometimes prayer is time spent simply gazing before the holy tabernacle ... *so I gaze on you in the sanctuary.* At other times one appreciates the grandeur of nature revealing *your strength and your glory.* Savouring the love of God is more precious than anything else... *your love is better than life.* The inner movements of prayer seek bodily expression as it expands into words of praise, gestures of blessing and the symbolic raising of hands. Our cultural conditioning has left us rather inhibited in giving bodily expression to prayer. The prayerful soul is filled as with a banquet and joy breaks out in song. Lying in bed at night, when the quieter parts of the mind can surface, this person is happy to remember God. *On you I muse through the night.*

Every part of life becomes a prayer for those who are thirsting for God. Their lamps are lit as they await the bridegroom.

For you my soul is thirsting, O God, my God.

THE GRACE OF WORKING
Psalm 127:1-5

The Old Testament is fond of repeating that the fear of God is the beginning of wisdom. This does not refer to that sort of cowering fear which fills one with dread, paralysing action, as happened to the servant in the parable who buried his talent because he was scared of his master. The fear of God which is a virtue means humble reverence before God and respect for God's laws. The psalmist sees this reverential fear as the foundation of happy and prosperous family life.

By the labour of your hands you shall eat.
You will be happy and prosper.

Humble reverence for God recognises the dignity of work. Developing one's talents shows an appreciation of what God has given. Saint Francis of Assisi, in his Rule of Life, wrote about the grace of working. At the opposite end of the spectrum, Ghandi listed wealth without work as one of the seven great sins of society. Today's first reading draws attention to the value of the everyday chores of housework. 'Let her works tell her praises at the city gates.'

The family home is the basic unit of society. The psalmist moves from the graces of the happy family to the wider society ... *in a happy Jerusalem.* The marriage ceremony emphasises that the Christian home is a blessing for society. Reverence for God, the development of one's talents and happy relationships are blessings to be desired far more than gold.

Indeed, thus shall be blessed
the one who fears the Lord.

A SERVANT KING
Psalm 22:1-3, 5-6

The choice of the shepherd-psalm for Christ the King is significant. He came, not to be served, but to serve. The kings of this
world are driven by the love of power but Jesus preferred the
power of love. Although he was Lord and master, yet he washed
the feet of the apostles. The gospel for the feast teaches that the
people who belong to his kingdom are those who follow his example of service in practical, everyday deeds of service.

The first reading, from Ezekiel, introduces the idea of the
shepherd as a caring leader, keeping his flock in view at all
times. Jesus took on this role of a shepherd at the service of his
flock.

The psalm celebrates many aspects of his loving service. As
the caring shepherd he is the one who satisfies our deepest
wants. He is the source of trustful repose. We meet him at the
wellsprings of prayer where he revives our drooping spirit. His
word guides us along the right path. As we travel though any
dark valley of life, he is always there as our support and protection. He feeds us on the banquet of bread from heaven, containing every delight and satisfying every taste. The bruises we suffer
from our scrapes and falls are anointed with the oil of his mercy.
He invites us to dwell in his own house forever. And the way
there is in following his call to serve one another in practical
charity.

Surely goodness and kindness shall follow me
all the days of my life.

STAY AWAKE
Psalm 79:2-3, 15-16, 18-19

Advent occurs when the days are at their darkest in the northern hemisphere. The word which dominates Advent prayer is 'Come'. God is ever coming towards us. As long as we have someone to whom we can say 'Come', we have hope. The liturgy of this winter season invites us to touch any darkness we may be experiencing in our own lives, or in the life of the church, or the society in which we live.

The psalm of the day was a prayer composed at a time of national trouble. The psalmist calls insistently on God ... *hear us ... shine forth ... rouse up your might ... come to our help ... turn again ... look down from heaven and see.*

The chosen vine represents the church. We ask the Lord to protect the church *which your right hand has planted.* O Lord, visit your church once more and may your hand be on those whom you have chosen to lead it.

Renewed in confidence, we promise that *we shall never forsake you again.* The purple of Advent is a reminder of the penitential aspect of the season. Penance calls for vigilance, staying awake, being on our guard against intruders who would steal our attention from the Lord who comes each day in life, in light and love. We prepare to welcome the Lord on his return by attending to his hidden presence today. Twice in today's gospel, at the beginning and the end, we are exhorted to stay awake, alert to his coming.

Let your face shine on us and we shall be saved.

WINTER WONDER
Psalm 84:8-14

It is a pity that Advent has been smothered by the extension of Christmas. The parties have begun, the Christmas music, lights and decorations are everywhere. The rich spirituality of Advent has been lost. Patrick Kavanagh began his poem, *Advent*, with a memorable couplet on the loss of wonder.

We have tested and tasted too much, lover –
Through a chink too wide there comes in no wonder.

Then he welcomes the therapy of a penitential Advent.

John the Baptist was a preacher of penance: penance to prepare the way for the Lord. I have long been fascinated by the lines in today's psalm:

Mercy and faithfulness have met;
justice and peace have embraced.
Faithfulness shall spring from the earth
and justice look down from heaven.

Justice is the necessary foundation of peace, yet justice on its own is not sufficient. Justice repairs what is broken and makes restitution for what is owed: but for the fullness of peace, it takes mercy and forgiveness to restore interpersonal relationships.

Isaiah, in today's first reading rejoiced that, after the exile, sin was atoned for, punishment had been endured. The defilements of the past were cleansed. The baptism of John involved repentance, voluntary acts of penance and a symbolic washing with water as reparation for sin. But more was needed and John prepared the way for someone coming ... coming with baptism of the Holy Spirit. The wonder of God's lovingkindness at Christmas will be appreciated most of all by those who acknowledge our need of a Saviour in a penitential Advent.

THE LORD IS NEAR
Luke 1:46-50, 53-54

It is Gaudete Sunday, when joy at the nearness of the Saviour is the dominant mood. It is celebrated especially in the extract from Saint Paul to the Thessalonians. 'Be happy at all times; pray constantly.'

Each year, the gospel readings for the Second and Third Sundays of Advent feature the preaching of John the Baptist. As the responsorial psalm we pray in the words of Mary's *Magnificat*. Mary's prayer belongs to the day of her visitation to Elizabeth, the joyful meeting of two people filled with God's Spirit. Mary can share the divine secret growing within her with Elizabeth who recognises Mary as the Mother of the Lord. The joy of the Lord's presence caused John the Baptist to dance in his mother's womb.

From the depths of Mary's soul wells up her canticle of praise.

My soul glorifies the Lord,
my spirit rejoices in God, my Saviour.

She sees herself as a nothingness made blessed by God's Spirit: an emptiness made fruitful with God's word. In the *Magnificat*, Mary anticipates the lesson of the beatitudes in the blessing of God on the poor and the reversal of the lot of the wealthy and powerful of this world.

He fills the starving with good things,
sends the rich away empty.

In our dark and empty experiences let us see in Mary a sign of what God's grace has done before and will do again. Take the advice of Paul: 'Be happy at all times; pray constantly.' Rejoice, for the Lord is near.

PROMISE AND FULFILMENT
Psalm 88:2-5, 27, 29

The importance of stories in the transmission of faith cannot be overestimated. When the great faith stories are no longer heard the culture of religious memory breaks down. In the wisdom of the yearly cycle the church continues to tell the great stories of Christmas, Easter and Pentecost as well as the lives of the saints. Faith is a personal response which flourishes more readily in a believing community. That is why it is said that faith is caught rather than taught.

Today's responsorial psalm is an example of memory being the bridge of hope between past promise and future fulfilment. The full psalm, one of the longest in the book, was composed after a sacking of Jerusalem by enemy forces dented the people's faith in God's promise. Towards the end of the psalm the question is raised: *Where are your mercies of the past, O Lord, which you have sworn in your faithfulness to David?* The psalmist's faith is not shaken because of his memory of the promise made to the house of David (today's first reading).

Of this I am sure, that your love lasts forever,
that your truth is firmly established as the heavens.

The day of fulfilment draws closer when Gabriel announces to Mary that her son will sit on the throne of David.

For all who travel in darkness of spirit, whose faith is tested, whose hope is wavering, may the Christmas story bring joy to their lives and a song to their hearts.

I will sing for ever of your love, O Lord.

The Reflections for the Feast of Christmas, the Holy Family, the Second Sunday of Christmas and the Epiphany are to be found in Cycle A.

THE WELLS OF SALVATION
Isaiah: 12:2-6

With joy you will draw water
from the wells of salvation.

The water table in Israel allows the sinking of wells in most parts of the country. No town or village would be built unless there was guaranteed access to water. Digging the well was usually a ceremonial process in which the participation of every family expressed the common ownership of the well. In the village, the well was the centre of community life, especially for the women for whom the well provided a daily meeting place. A popular book of the 1960s, *The Ugly American*, recounted the disastrous social effects of replacing the well in a village with modern piping and taps. It reads as a parable applicable to many dubious products of what is regarded as progress.

John's gospel is especially sensitive to the importance of wells. It was there that Jesus met the Samaritan woman, the man paralysed for thirty-eight years and the man blind from birth. The Feast of Tabernacles celebrated the protection of God during the tented days of the Exodus. A special celebration with water recalled the miracle of water from the rock to save the people. At that celebration Jesus applied the invitation of Isaiah to himself. 'Let anyone who is thirsty come to me! Let anyone who believes in me come and drink!' (Jn 7:37-38).

It was fitting that the public ministry of Jesus began at his baptism. And that Christian life also begins at the well of salvation.

With joy you will draw water
from the wells of salvation.

THE FIRST COVENANT
Psalm 24:4-9. R/ v 10

For the Sundays in Ordinary Time the Old Testament reading is chosen for its thematic connection with the gospel, but in Lent, Easter and Advent and Christmas, the first reading has no deliberate connection with the gospel. The psalm of the day is chosen as a response to the first reading. This year, the readings from the Old Testament trace the history of God's covenant with the chosen people.

The first covenant was the promise made by God to Noah not to destroy the world. The people's side of the contract was to avoid the sinful ways which brought about the punishment of the flood. The fusion of the colours of the rainbow, the components of white light, is taken as a sign of the covenant.

The verses of the psalm are prayed in response to God's covenant of protection.

Your ways, Lord, are faithfulness and love
for those who keep your covenant.

God's faithfulness is sure, but our faithfulness is tested in the struggles and temptations of life. The temptations of Jesus may be understood as clarifying his mind about the way he would proceed in his ministry. The wiles of Satan are unmasked. We pray for God's clarifying light.

Lord, make me know your ways.
Lord, teach me your paths.

For our past infidelities we turn to God's mercy.

Remember your mercy, Lord,
and the love you have shown from of old.

'Repent and believe in the Good News.' May our Lent be a journey towards greater fidelity.

ABRAHAM, MODEL OF FAITH
Psalm 115:10, 15-19. R/ Ps 114:9

The second revelation of God's covenant was made to Abraham. Abraham's life is the pattern of the pilgrimage of faith. He goes beyond the confines of home life, on the strength of God's word, on a journey towards an unseen land. This journey takes him through a series of ten blessings and seven trials. The greatest blessings are promises of a multitude of descendants while the most severe trial is the prospect of slaying Isaac, his only son and heir. When little Isaac (meaning the smile of God) asks about the lamb for the sacrifice, Abraham bravely answers, 'God will provide.' Because of the greatness of his trust, Abraham is rewarded with a renewal of God's blessed promise.

Today's psalm-response makes use of verses from two psalms. From Psalm 114 we respond to the blessings of the light of faith:

I will walk in the presence of the Lord
in the land of the living.

Then in three verses from Psalm 115 we express the trials of life:

I trusted, even when I said:
I am sorely afflicted.

At the transfiguration of Jesus, three disciples received the strengthening of a great blessing. But on the way down from the mountain Jesus spoke to them about his forthcoming death and resurrection. As the bread is blessed before it is broken, the servant of God is strengthened before trials come.

We journey towards Easter with a renewed understanding of the rhythm of blessing and testing, of light and darkness in the pilgrimage of faith.

I will walk in the presence of the Lord
in the land of the living.

THE COMMANDMENTS
Psalm 18: 8-11. R/ Jn 6:68

God's covenant with the people was first given to Noah and later developed with Abraham. Today's reading from the Old Testament brings us to the specification of the charter in the commandments given to Moses after God had liberated the people from slavery in Egypt.

For the Hebrew people the revelation of God did not come in philosophical reflection or in mystical oracles but through God's covenant expressed in the law. God revealed the rules of life and worship. If they observed these precepts they would enjoy God's special protection. The law was like a protecting fence. Outside it lay danger and destruction, but by staying within its confines they were promised peace and prosperity. It was considered the greatest boon of leisure to have time to ponder the law.

The psalm responds to the gift of God's guidance in the commandments. *The Law of the Lord is perfect. It revives the soul. It gives wisdom to the simple and light to the eyes. It is more to be desired than gold, sweeter than honey.*

A narrowminded reverence for the law produced the extreme of a withering legalism which Jesus attacked, but that is no excuse to go to the opposite extreme of disregarding religious laws. Authority and obedience are out of fashion in this permissive age. Today's liturgy invites us to ponder on the wisdom of the commandments as a light on life.

The decalogue gives three directives on divine worship, five basic laws for family and society, and two on internal self-control.

You, Lord, have the message of eternal life.

EXILE IN BABYLON
Psalm 136:1-6

The fourth act in the story of the covenant is an unhappy one. The reading from Second Chronicles recalls the infidelities and shameful practices of the people, and how God's messengers were ridiculed, until there was no further remedy. Having disregarded the covenant, their temple was destroyed, their land taken, and they were deported to Babylon.

The psalm picks up the sadness of the exiles *by the rivers of Babylon*. Many of the exiles abandoned their belief in God's intervention and protection, but a faithful remnant persevered in their hope of returning to the land which they believed that God had once given to them.

This well-known psalm is the classic elegy of any soul feeling alienated from God for whatever reason. The images in the psalm are vivid and poignant. The rivers of that strange land were swollen by their tears. The tapering poplars served as lofty perches for harps no longer plucked in joy. *O how could we sing the song of the Lord on alien soil?*

Perhaps we can relate the psalm to our situation today. In a secularised society, those who remain faithful to God's precepts sometimes feel like exiles in a foreign land. The writer of 2 Chronicles compares the exile to a sabbath rest necessary to purify the land. The happy news is that the exile ended in a glorious return to Jerusalem. And the gospel and second reading of today remind us of God's love for us.

'God loved the world so much
that he gave his only Son' (Jn 3:16).

A NEW HEART
Psalm 50:3-4, 12-15

The exile in Babylon marked the disintegration of the covenant of God with the people. In today's reading we hear the Lord speaking through Jeremiah: 'They broke that covenant of mine, so I had to show them who was master.' But a new covenant is promised. 'Deep within them I will plant my Law, writing it in their hearts. Then I will be their God and they shall be my people.'

The psalm of David's repentance is the perfect response to the reading. He too recognises his need for a new heart as he turns away from his shameful infidelities.

A pure heart create for me, O God,
put a steadfast spirit within me.
Do not cast me away from your presence,
nor deprive me of your holy spirit.

In contrast to the darkness of his offences, the words he uses about God refer to kindness, compassion, cleansing and joy. He prays for *the joy of your help* and *a spirit of fervour* to sustain him so that he may be an inspiration to other sinners to return to God.

Today's reading from Hebrews teaches that Jesus submitted so humbly that his prayer was heard. The humble repentance of the sinner is like the seed decaying in the ground before the new life flourishes.

An honest and humble confession is the best preparation for celebrating Easter's new covenant, new heart and new life.

'And when I am lifted up from the earth,
I shall draw all people to myself.'

FORSAKEN
Psalm 21:8-9, 17-20, 23-24. R/ v 2

Mark's version of the passion is the most violent and brutal of any of the gospels. He portrays Jesus dying in utter dereliction quoting this psalm in a heart-rending cry:

My God, my God, why have you forsaken me?

The psalm reads like a descriptive commentary on the scene on Calvary. We see the mocking crowd, curling their lips and tossing their heads. We hear their taunts: 'He saved others, he cannot save himself.' We hear the clanging of hammer on nails, tearing open the wounds on hands and feet. Like bloodthirsty dogs, they yell for his blood. His body is stretched so that one can count the bones in his rib cage. His clothing is divided, his outer garment the prize of a lottery.

Yet the psalmist finds hope in this awful situation when he turns to God. God will not leave him deserted but will renew his strength. And his future joy will be in witnessing to God's power seen most clearly in his suffering. So it happened that, it was on seeing how Jesus died, the centurion recognised the presence of God in the events of that day.

You who fear the Lord give him praise;
all sons of Jacob give him glory.
Revere him, Israel's sons.

The reflections for Easter Sunday, the Second Sunday of Easter, the Ascension of the Lord and Pentecost are to be found in Cycle A.

NIGHT PRAYER
Psalm 4:2, 4, 7, 9

Every Sunday is a little Easter as Christians gather in the memory of the risen Lord. So it is appropriate that the Night Prayer of the church for Saturday should use Psalm 4, as it were, entering the sleep of Christ between his death and his rising.

It is a grand form of prayer to relax with the Lord at the end of the day to review the happenings of the day. This psalm is a model of what we need to touch.

I will lie down in peace and sleep comes at once. Two of the greatest obstacles to sleep are unresolved business from the past and anxiety about the morrow. Shakespeare's Macbeth, burdened with a guilty conscience, envied innocent sleep,

'*sleep that knits up the ravel'd sleave of care,*
the death of each day's life, sore labour's bath,
balm of hurt minds ...'

From anguish you released me. I need to thank God for helping me through the day. Were there any particular situations of stress? Anguish? Pain? Frustration? Moments when anger began to bubble? It was God's help, perhaps unnoticed at the time, which carried me through.

Have mercy and hear me. Did I fail God today? Hurt anybody? Compromised my principles?

What can bring us happiness? What were the good moments today? When did I feel a deep contentment? Did the Lord *lift up the light of his face on us?*

A good night's sleep brings great peace.
I will lie down in peace and sleep comes at once,
for you alone, Lord, make me dwell in safety.

VOCATION TO MISSION
Psalm 117:1, 8-9, 21-23, 26, 28-29

The stone which the builders rejected
has become the cornerstone.

In today's reading from Acts, Peter compares the raising of Jesus from the dead to the choosing of a rejected stone to become the honoured cornerstone. The psalm picks up the theme.

This is the work of the Lord, a marvel in our eyes.

This psalm was sung at the enthronement of a new king. The new ruler, added to the line of kings, is represented as a decorative cornerstone added to a wall which awaited completion. Peter, however, sees the stone not only as an ornamental cornice but also as the keystone which clamps the adjoining walls together. The greater the pressure, the more tightly bound is the structure.

The idea is appropriate for Vocations Sunday when we recognise that the mission of the church is not yet complete and we pray for people to answer the call to ministry. In the First Letter of Peter, he again speaks of Jesus as the keystone and he extends the image to Christians, exhorting them to become living stones forming a spiritual house and holy priesthood.

Today, Vocations Sunday, we encourage people to hear the call of God to take up a more active role in the apostolate. The church is alive where people are actively involved. We may feel unworthy, but the past is no obstacle in the eyes of God who can do marvels with the stone that was once cast aside.

Give thanks to the Lord for he is good;
for his love has no end.

BRANCHES OF THE VINE
Psalm 21:26-28, 30-32

Great are the works of the Lord! Today's responsorial verses are taken from the psalm which begins with the cry of Jesus on the cross: *My God, my God, why have you forsaken me?* But hope is a wonderful gift. The darkness of despair is lifted and the psalmist recalls the goodness of God who has heard his cry. He resolves to commit his life to God's service. *My vows I will pay before those who fear him.* Furthermore, he will pass on the story to his children who will tell it to the next generation.

They shall tell of the Lord to generations yet to come,
declare his faithfulness to peoples yet unborn.

If the psalmist hadn't experienced such darkness in the past he would not now appreciate God's saving action as much. He has been through the school of suffering. There he learnt a deeper appreciation of God's faithfulness. Light is more appreciated by those who knew the darkness. The vine which bears most fruit is the one which suffered a severe pruning. It is the most fragile part which bears the fruit. Many of those who bore fruit in the Lord's service were vulnerable people who were conscious of their past failures. Moses had murdered a man. David's moment of lust instigated a whole train of evil deeds. Peter denied his contact with Jesus. Paul once persecuted the followers of Jesus.

The great secret of working in God's service is keeping contact with home. And home is Jesus Christ.

These things the Lord has done ... but apart from me you can do nothing.

A NEW SONG OF SALVATION
Psalm 97:1-4

Having listened to a reading from the Acts, in which Peter comes to recognise that the message of salvation is not just for his fellow Jews but for all nations, we respond in a psalm which celebrates that universal salvation.

The Lord has made known his salvation;
has shown his justice to the nations.

Originally it was an enthronement psalm, sung at the coronation of a new king in Israel. They understood that their permission to have an earthly king was always subject to the universal dominion of God. At the enthronement ceremony they prayed that a good king in Israel would manifest God's justice before all nations.

All the ends of the earth have seen
the salvation of our God.

The story of salvation attained a new meaning in the life of divine intimacy that Jesus spoke about. In today's gospel the Lord offers to share his love, his joy, his friendship, his knowledge and his fruitfulness with his disciples. This is a covenant that is entirely new and it calls for a new song.

Sing a new song to the Lord
for he has worked wonders.

Each day is a new day of divine intimacy. Each prayer is a new prayer. Every time the song is sung the music is new. The mystery of the Lord's saving deeds is newly alive in every celebration of the Eucharist, done in memory of him. It is good news that we should shout aloud that all might hear.

Shout aloud to the Lord all the earth, ring out your joy.

THANKS FOR THE MEMORY
Psalm 102:1-2, 11-12, 19-20

When family and friends gather after the departure of a loved one from this life, I have always found them recalling memories of the one who has gone. I imagine the apostles and Mary recalling incidents and stories of Jesus. They would have recognised how privileged they were to have seen and heard so much. Thanksgiving would have been part of their prayer.

My soul, give thanks to the Lord
and never forget all his blessings.

Taking today's psalm verses as guide, we can highlight three divine blessings they had witnessed in the life of Jesus.

For as the heavens are high above the earth
so strong is his love for those who fear him.

In the life of Jesus they had seen divine love clad in human flesh: love that never gets embittered, is always ready to forgive, and generous to the point of total self-sacrifice. 'As long as we love one another,' writes John, 'God will live in us and his love will be complete in us.'

As far as the east is from the west
so far does he remove our sins.

In Jesus they had seen the Lamb of God who takes away the sins of the world.

His kingdom is ruling over all.

In the ministry of Jesus they had seen Satan cast out, evil conquered and the reign of God offered to all people. They were called to be workers in the kingdom. Full of hope, they waited for the promised power from on high.

Come, Holy Spirit, renew the face of the earth.

THE ONE TRUE GOD
Psalm 32:4-6, 9, 18-20, 22

Christian belief in the Blessed Trinity, one God in three persons, came at the end of a long development of religious thought. The first important step was when the Israelites recognised the specialness of their God above all other gods ... a great God above all gods. Gradually this God was seen as the only true God. In today's reading from Deuteronomy, Moses asks the Israelites to recognise how blessed they were as a people chosen for the revelation of this one God. 'The Lord is God indeed, in heaven above as on earth beneath, he and no other.'

Picking up this theme is a beautiful psalm to God whose power is awesome in creation, yet whose faithful love *fills the earth*. God's power is so great that it was *by his word the heavens were made, by the breath of his mouth all the stars*. The gods of the pagans tended to be cruel, conniving and capricious, but the God of the Bible is one who loves his people. Even when they stray into sinful ways, God's look is tender. He reaches down *to rescue their souls from death, to keep them alive in famine*.

The psalmist anticipates a greater coming of God: *Our soul is waiting for God*. We are in the happy position of recognising that coming in the incarnation of God the Son, the Word made flesh.

In prayer we open our lives to receive the fullness of his Spirit of love.

May your love be upon us, O Lord,
as we place all our hope in you.

THE BLOOD OF THE COVENANT
Psalm 115:12-13, 15-18

The Sundays of Lent in this year's cycle traced the stages of God's covenant with the people. Today's liturgy celebrates the new covenant ratified in the blood of Christ. The responsorial psalm is a prayer of gratitude and promise to God and it serves as a prayerful response to three readings which focus on the ratification of the covenant by the shedding of blood.

When Jesus took the cup and said, 'This is my blood, the blood of the covenant, which is to be poured out for many', he was bringing to fulfilment what had been prefigured in several ways. The Passover, which they were celebrating, recalled the blood of the lamb sprinkled on the Hebrews' doors to save them from the destroying angel. When Moses assembled the people to ratify God's covenant with them, he sacrificed animals and sprinkled the life-blood over the people. The blood of animals was shed in atonement for sin, as today's reading from Hebrews recalls. Jesus was effectively saying: 'Come and receive me. I am the Paschal Lamb whose blood liberates you from slavery, frees you from sin and ratifies the new covenant which makes you children of God.'

The psalmist asks: *How can I repay the Lord for his goodness to me?* Jesus invites us to participate in his self-offering to the Father, the one, perfect sacrifice. *Precious* is his death which has *loosened my bonds.* The word *eucharist* means giving thanks ... *a thanksgiving sacrifice I will make.*

The cup of salvation I will raise:
I will call on the Lord's name.

AT HOME IN HIS WORD
Psalm 39:2, 4, 7-10

Samuel offered an open ear to hear the call of God ... 'and let no word of his fall to the ground.' The psalm picks up this theme of obedience. *Here I am, Lord, I come to do your will.* Hebrews applies these words to Jesus coming into the world. Obedience to the Father is a very prominent theme in John's gospel. Today's extract from John is the reader's first encounter with Jesus in that gospel. Two of the Baptist's disciples asked Jesus, 'Where do you live?' His reply was an invitation: 'Come and see.' The local address of Jesus' lodgings is of no concern to the evangelist. Ultimately he leads the reader to see that Jesus is really at home in perfect union with the Father. 'I am in the Father and the Father is in me' (Jn 14:11). And where Jesus lives is where the disciple strives to be. 'If you make my word your home you will indeed be my disciples' (Jn 8:31).

Obedience begins in hearing. In fact, the word, *obedience*, comes from the Latin word for listening. It is a virtue that does not rest easily with the modern mind which sets so much store on personal liberty as a priority. We are the people of the me-generation.

My God, I delight in your law in the depth of my heart. Can I, in all truth, say that the deepest delight of my life is in seeking what God wants? Or is it always my own agenda?

Here I am, Lord, I come to do your will.

THE GOOD NEWS
Psalm 24:4-9

Today's gospel launches Jesus on his public ministry. He proclaimed the good news that the time had come for the reign of God on earth. The implication was that up till then people had yielded to the reign of the devil. Jesus instructed his listeners to repent and believe the good news. The word, *repent,* literally means to think again, *repensare.* Jesus offered the world a new way of seeing, a new system of values and a new standard of loving.

The psalm chosen to accompany this gospel reading is a prayer that God, in his mercy and love, would teach us his ways.

Lord, make me know your ways.

Lord, teach me your paths.

Make me walk in your truth and teach me:

for you are God my saviour.

Jesus called the fishermen to leave their boats and follow him. To become a follower demands more than subscribing to a set of doctrines or moral principles. To believe means, above all, to give one's heart to the Lord in a personal relationship. It means to walk the road of life in the company of the Lord, to think with his mind and to act out of his values.

In his letter for the beginning of the new millennium, Pope John Paul II offered no magic formula for the problems and challenges of our age. 'No,' he wrote, 'we shall not be saved by a formula but by a Person, and the assurance which he gives us: *I am with you.*' The essence of the good news is Jesus, the Saviour, risen and with us.

HE SPOKE WITH AUTHORITY
Psalm 94:1-2, 6-9

In today's gospel Jesus began to teach. He spoke with authority. Maybe it means that he spoke from personal experience, unlike the preachers who were content to quote from others. But authority also refers to the presence of God's power in his words. This authority is the divine power which he revealed in casting out the noisy, unclean spirit from the possessed man.

Notice that the first words Jesus said were, 'Be quiet.' The psalm is an invitation to come to pray. We are invited to kneel and bend low before the God who made us. Prayer lifts up the mind and heart beyond the noisy clamours of our small world to the great and timeless presence of God. The psalm recalls that God is maker of all and has called us to be the chosen people of his flock. Then we are told to listen to his voice ... just as Jesus told the possessed man to be quiet.

How and where can we listen to his voice? God speaks to us in many ways ... in nature, good reading, the teaching of the church, good example etc., but especially in sacred scripture. It is called the word of God and it is invested with divine authority, that is, the presence and power of God.

At the conclusion of a liturgical reading from scripture we hear: 'This is the word of the Lord.' Do I really believe this? Do I find the presence and power of God in the word? Must I learn how to be quiet?

O that today you would listen to his voice!

THE SOURCE OF HEALING
Psalm 146:1-6

The gospel of the day shows Jesus healing many people but also taking time to attend to his own inner need of prayer. Early in the morning, before the demands of the day pressed in on his inner space, he went to the lonely place to pray there. The best way to groom ourselves for the tasks of the day is before the mirror of prayer. It prepares us to live the day close to the Lord. I heard a preacher say ... with a grain of humour ... that a person busy in ministry needs an hour each day in prayer, the very busy person needs two hours, while the unbusy person doesn't need much time. Who heals the healers? Who ministers to the ministers?

The psalm expresses the praise that is due to God as the source of all ministry and healing. *To him our praise is due.*

It is important to remember that in praying any psalm I am never on my own. Psalms are community prayers which we recite on behalf of the entire people of God. In praying this psalm today, Jerusalem represents the church. We are asking that the Lord will build up the church so damaged in recent times: that the exiles, those who have drifted away from religious practice, will return to their baptismal homeland: that the broken-hearted will find healing: and that all emotional wounds will receive proper attention.

Praise the Lord for he is good;
sing to our God for he is loving;
to him our praise is due.

THE LEPROSY OF SIN
Psalm 31:1-2, 5, 11

The gospel and first reading are about the plight of one affected with leprosy. The psalm is about the leprosy of sin. *Happy the one whose offence is forgiven, whose sin is remitted.*

Leprosy is a disease that first attacks the outer skin and then devours the inner structure of the afflicted part. It is an apt image of sin ... how the gradual slide into the pattern of sin eats away at inner dignity and self-respect. The gradual descent into the state of sin was described by the shepherd who says that the lost sheep nibbled its way lost.

As the first reading shows, to avoid the spread of the disease, the leper was compelled to leave family and society. This alienation from family is an image of the sinner's alienation from God. He/she is full of guile in denying the truth ... and rebels against God and church. In the mission of Jesus, divine power broke into the world to establish the reign of God. He came with a new healing power. He reached towards the outcast. 'He touched him, and the leprosy left him at once.' In like manner he reached out to the sinner. He did not come to condemn but to restore hope and life.

Our psalm today celebrates the wonders of divine mercy. Our part is to acknowledge our sins in humble confession. *My guilt I did not hide.* What a relief it is to have our sins forgiven and our dignity restored.

Happy the one whose offence is forgiven
whose sin is remitted.

HEALED IN SOUL AND BODY
Psalm 40:2-5, 13-14

Today's readings recognise the link that often exists between mental or spiritual problems and physical ailments. Sometimes healing of the spirit is necessary before physical healing can occur. Jesus first offered the crippled man forgiveness of his sins before his physical healing. Layers of roofing, then layers of negativity and guilt had to be stripped away. The physical symptoms are sometimes the presenting case for the spiritual problem. Then notice the firmness of voice when Jesus ordered him to stand up, take up his stretcher and walk. The physical ailment will come back if there is not a new, positive mental approach. That tallies with the firm purpose of amendment which is a necessary part of confessing sinfulness.

In the psalm we find a similar connection of the easing of pain with the forgiveness of guilt.

The Lord will help him on his bed of pain,
he will bring him back from sickness to health.
As for me, I said: 'Lord, have mercy on me,
heal my soul for I have sinned against you.'

God is ever ready to forgive our sins. We are then asked to stand up and walk in newness of spirit. Prayer and fasting are good remedies. But better still are acts of kindness and generosity because these reveal the inner healing and a new, positive attitude. Charity covers a multitude.

Happy the person who considers the poor and the weak.
The Lord will save him in the day of evil.

CELEBRATING MERCY
Psalm 102:1-4, 8, 10, 12-13

There is a time to fast and a time to celebrate: a time to confess sins and a time to celebrate mercy. It is often said that Catholics have been taught how to confess but not how to bless. The emphasis in today's liturgy is on praising God for his blessings.

The image of a people drawn into marriage with God occurs in the gospel and the reading from Hosea. Hosea's personal experience of the humiliation of having an unfaithful wife became a parable of the chosen people who were unfaithful to God's covenant. The good news is that God's love remains faithful and will lure the nation into a new marriage: 'I will betroth you to myself forever.' This reading prepares us for Jesus speaking of his time among the people as a wonderful marriage of God and people. And such a wedding is no time for patched up garments, dried up wineskins or penitential fasting. Jesus wanted his disciples to celebrate the blessings of divine fidelity and mercy. That is why the wisdom of the church asks for more than the private confessing of sins: we are encouraged to celebrate mercy in a special sacrament.

The psalm of the day captures this mood of celebrating divine mercy. It contains gems of prayer which we treasure in memory.

The Lord is compassion and love, slow to anger and rich in mercy.
So far as the east is from the west so far does he remove our sins.
My soul, give thanks to the Lord and never forget all his blessings.

A DAY OF SACRED MEMORY
Psalm 80:3-8, 10-11

The observance of the sabbath comes up in the first reading and the gospel. The psalm is a call to celebrate a feast to remember God's saving deeds.

A voice I did not know said to me:

I freed your shoulder from the burden;

The first thing to be called holy in the Bible was a day ... the seventh day when God rested from labour to contemplate his works. Today's reading from Deuteronomy sees the sabbath as a day of rest for the servants, reminding the people that they were servants in Egypt. The gospel deals with the manner of celebrating the sabbath. The man with the withered hand was a symbol of an excessively legal and negative approach which had withered the joy of celebrating. 'The sabbath was made for man, not man for the sabbath.' The sacred day of rest serves basic human needs. It is a time each week to foster our relationship with God and with family, while also giving space and attention to our own deeper selves. Basically, it is a day to cultivate memory. Memory is at the heart of liturgy. 'Do this in memory of me.' The psalm of the day remembers the liberation of the people.

It is ironic that in this age of labour-saving devices we seem to have less time and more stress. There is great healing power in memory, especially sacred memory. Time with the Lord on the sacred day can allow the healing of the withered arm.

Ring out your joy to God our strength.

THE DEPTHS OF CONFUSION
Psalm 129

The psalm that begins 'Out of the depths', *De Profundis*, is usually associated with praying for the dead. What is its connection with the first reading and gospel today? The depths refer to the darkness of mind and dryness of spirit that afflict the confused soul.

After falling to the serpent's subtle temptation Adam appears to be lost. God calls out to him, 'Adam, where are you?' It is not as if God does not know where he is, but does Adam know? The great adversary (which is the meaning of Satan) leads one off the path of truth and into the depths of confusion. Another name for the tempter is *diabolos* (devil). The etymology of this word is significant. In Greek, *diabolos* is the opposite of symbol. In a symbol there is a movement of meanings leading to unity of thought. The opposite movement is towards confusion of thought. *The Catechism of the Catholic Church* calls the devil (*diabolos*) 'the one who throws himself across God's plan and the work of salvation accomplished in Christ.'

Mark's gospel speaks of the confused relatives of Jesus who were convinced that he was out of his mind, possibly under an evil influence. No wonder Jesus called the devil the father of lies. And the most effective lie is the half-truth.

This psalm can be a prayer for anybody confused in faith ... tempted ... struggling in the depths of guilt ... pleading in the desert of aridity ... longing for the daybreak during the night of faith.

Out of the depths I cry to you, O Lord.

PALM-TREES AND CEDARS
Psalm 91:2-3, 13-16

Jesus drew parables from the familiar world to explain the mysteries of God's grace. A mustard seed is a tiny, yellow specimen, scarcely bigger than a speck of dust. Yet it has a potential for growth that the dust does not contain. A seed is a symbol of hope.

Ezekiel's image of hope in the first reading is nothing tiny but he opts for the mighty cedar of Lebanon. The following psalm is a joyful hymn of thanksgiving to God which takes two trees, the palm and cedar, as images of hope for the people.

The palm tree is a symbol of prayer because of its shape. It grows tall, putting out no branches until it spreads out at the top in drooping fronds which are fruit-bearing. It represents the stance of prayer, upraised directly towards heaven, spreading arms in supplication. The palm is very valuable for its timber, its nutritious fruit and its oil.

A friend who knows my love of trees gave me a little cedar of Lebanon as a gift to honour a jubilee. It is spreading into a beautiful tree, though in our climate it will never attain the massive size of the biblical specimens. The cedar produces timber long-lasting for building and it has the added value of a most pleasant aroma. Once we had a problem with dampness in a tabernacle but an inner frame of cedar solved the problem. We can make the psalmist's optimism our own:

The just will flourish like the palm-tree
and grow like a Lebanon cedar.

CALMING THE STORM
Psalm 106:23-26, 28-31

Today's psalm is from a ceremony in the temple where the priest invited various people to offer witness to God's power coming to their rescue in times of distress. After hearing the testimony of people rescued from the desert, from gloomy prison and from sickness, the fourth testimony concerns rescue from the terrors of a storm at sea.

These men have seen the Lord's deeds,
the wonders he does in the deep.

It is an obvious section of a psalm to accompany Mark's account of Jesus calming the storm at sea.

The Jews of biblical times were uncomfortable with the sea. They were never known as great sailors. The wild sea reminded them of the primitive chaos which had to be controlled by God at the creation of the world. It was considered the abode of evil spirits. This accounts for the way Jesus rebuked the sea as in an exorcism and gave the same order as in the healing of a possessed man: 'Quiet now! Be calm!'

The storm-tossed boat is a metaphor of the plight of the church in recent times. What is reassuring is the power of Jesus over the storm.

Returning to the background of the psalm we are encouraged to set the present plight of the church into the wider context of history. The times of lowest morale produced the greatest saints and reformers.

Then they cried to the Lord in their need
and he rescued them from their distress.
He stilled the storm to a whisper:
and the waves of the sea were hushed.

POWER TO RESTORE
Psalm 29:2, 4-6, 11-13

Today's gospel relates two stories which show the power of Jesus to save a life that was wasting away and even to restore life to the girl who had died. The first reading tells us that death was not God's doing and that God takes no pleasure in the extinction of the living. The psalm is a very explicit response to this God who rescues and restores.

O Lord, you have raised my soul from the dead,
restored me to life from those who sink into the grave.

The heading over this psalm in the Bible associates it with the dedication of the temple after it had been desecrated by foreign invaders ... *you have not let my enemies rejoice over me.* The psalmist reflects on the way that our problems may seem to have no way out when we are going through them, but divine intervention can change everything in no time at all.

His anger lasts but a moment; his favour though life.
At night there are tears, but joy comes with dawn.

We live at a time when many people have lost the larger picture of life: life has become a meaningless succession of disassociated moments. As a result, they do not think with a timescale that allows darkness wait until dawn. The resurrection of Jesus was the greatest act of rescue. It gives Christianity an essentially optimistic mentality. Faith enables one to reach out and touch the Lord who rescues and restores.

For me you have changed my mourning into dancing.

LOOKING UP
Psalm 122

Rejection is an experience suffered by Ezekiel, Paul and Jesus in today's readings. We read of rebels who are defiant and obstinate, of insults and persecutions, and of the prophet who is despised in his own country. The psalm is an echo of these negative experiences.

We are filled with contempt.
Indeed all too full is our soul
with the scorn of the rich,
with the proud man's disdain.

This psalm is one of the collection called songs of ascent which were chanted by pilgrims going up the temple hill in procession. It is easy to think of prayer as a going up ... the elevation of the heart and mind to God, as the classical definition puts it.

To you have I lifted up my eyes,
You who dwell in the heavens.

The heart of prayerfulness is attentiveness to God. The psalmist pictures the eyes of the slave fixed on the master's hand, the eyes of the servant-girl on the hand of her mistress. The attentive servant can take direction from the slightest nod or glance. This is a beautiful example of the sensitivity of the prayerful soul to God's presence and direction ... *so our eyes are on the Lord our God.*

The psalmist prays in the name of all who are victims of rejection, contempt and scorn. His advice is to look beyond the problems, to raise up one's eyes to God above, confident that his mercy will prevail.

Our eyes are on the Lord
till he show us his mercy.

A VOICE THAT SPEAKS OF PEACE
Psalm 84:9-14

The readings feature the call of Amos and the apostles to the mission of proclaiming the word of God. Amos responded to God's call and became a scathing critic of the selfish use of wealth. Verbs of mission, like *go* or *send*, occur more than two hundred times in the gospels. The mission of the word extends far beyond personal salvation. It is a call to take on the ethics of responsibility for the betterment of society. In the face of the rampant individualism of today, Pope John Paul II wrote that the great challenge facing the church at the beginning of the third millennium is to be the home and school of communion.

The psalmist resolves to listen to the call of the Lord. *I will hear what the Lord God has to say*. The message that he hears concerns working for peace ... *a voice that speaks of peace*. The task of making peace is not confined to the political leaders of the world. Civil leaders depend to a great extent on public opinion.

Mercy, faithfulness, justice and peace are pictured by the psalmist as rapt in the one embrace. Mercy moves beyond vengeance. Vengeance might achieve equal retribution but it will not restore personal relationships. Mercy can heal the hurts.

Fidelity is the foundation of trustfulness. There can be no prospect of peace without the structures of justice. When mercy, faithfulness and justice embrace, then peace has every chance of blossoming.

If we *hear what the Lord God has to say*, we will work responsibly for justice and peace.

RESTFUL WATERS
Psalm 22

The choice of the popular shepherd-psalm is most appropriate on a Sunday when the readings speak of God's compassion for a straying people under the image of the shepherd leading and pasturing his flock. 'He took pity on them because they were like sheep without a shepherd.'

Let us concentrate on one aspect of the shepherd's service.

Near restful waters he leads me,
to revive my drooping spirit.

In the land of the Bible, sheep pastured on the rocky mountainsides, allowing the more fertile valleys for growing crops and vines. In contrast to other animals, sheep require very little water. Any water on the mountainside is cascading rapidly downhill. Sheep find it very difficult to drink from flowing water, so the shepherd has to find or make a pool of still water for them. The flowing water is an image of our racing time. Although we believe that God is everywhere, we find it difficult to drink of God's presence when the pace of life is too hectic. We need the pool of still time to revive our drooping spirits and flagging faith.

It was a lesson Jesus gave to the apostles. After a period of action he called them to come apart to a quiet place where they could be by themselves. There is no mention of any lectures for them ... just quietness, rest and time to be by themselves. Unless we periodically come apart we run the risk of being torn apart.

Near restful waters he leads me,
to revive my drooping spirit.

YOU GIVE THEM FOOD
Psalm 144:10-11, 15-18

Today we commence five Sundays when the gospel is taken from John's chapter on the bread of life. He begins with the miraculous provision of food to feed the physical hunger of people. The multiplication of the loaves and fishes was foreshadowed in Elisha's day by the provision of sufficient food for a hundred men from twenty barley loaves. 'Give it to the people to eat.'

The accompanying psalm is a hymn of gratitude to God in which each successive letter of the Hebrew alphabet starts a verse. The verses chosen for today form a beautiful grace before meals.

The eyes of all creatures look to you
and you give them their food in due time.

That's a most appealing picture. In my mind's eye I can see a little child, saying nothing, but with open eyes pleading to mother, 'I'd love a lick of what you are baking.' Merely to look in confidence towards God is a total prayer. Words are not necessary. The Lord is not stinting in his response. His hands are opened wide.

But may we pray this psalm with a clear conscience if so many people are living without sufficient food while our pampered society suffers from overindulgence? God asks the wealthy nations to share their providential resources just as Jesus asked his disciples to distribute the bread he had provided.

The Lord is just in all his ways ... are we?
The Lord is loving in all his deeds ... are we?
The Lord opens wide his hand ... do we?

THE BREAD OF THE WORD
Psalm 77:3-4, 23-25, 54

Psalm 77 is a long recital of the events of salvation history from Jacob to David. From one generation to the next, *the things we have heard and understood, the things our fathers have told us, we will tell to the next generation; the glories of the Lord and his might.* The deeds of God are passed on in word.

The verses selected today harmonise with the first reading and the gospel by recalling the miracle of the manna.

He rained down manna for their food,
and gave them bread from heaven.

After Jesus gave people bread for the body, the people came back for more. Jesus wants them to move on from there. He speaks of the material bread as a sign. A signpost on the road is an indicator of the direction in which we are to proceed. Where Jesus wants them to proceed is into believing in his word. 'I am the bread of life. He who comes to me will never be hungry; he who believes in me will never thirst.' His words here are an echo of the words of Ben Sirach about desiring the gift of divine wisdom. The first part of the Mass is celebrated at the table of the word because Jesus is the bread come down from heaven, first of all, in the sense that his word is the food of faith.

As noted above, the long psalm of salvation history was a recital of God's saving actions, passing on the story that people might believe and give glory to God.

Mere men ate the bread of angels.

BREAD FOR THE JOURNEY
Psalm 33:2-9

This is an alphabetical psalm in which the successive verses commence with the letters of the Hebrew alphabet in sequence. God is praised, blessed and glorified, the object of boasting and the source of gladness. God has answered the psalmist's prayer for deliverance.

I sought the Lord and he answered me;
from all my terrors he set me free.

This psalm might well have expressed the sentiments of Elijah after his experience in the wilderness.

The angel of the Lord is encamped
around those who revere him to rescue them.

The angel who touched Elijah in his depressed sleep gave him water to drink and a hot scone to eat.

Taste and see that the Lord is good.
He is happy who seeks refuge in him.

And in the strength of that food, Elijah found the energy to walk for forty days and forty nights to the holy mountain where he met the Lord in the gentle breeze.

This bread for the journey which Elijah tasted was a wonderful anticipation of the bread of life that Jesus would give. As we progress with John's gospel, there is an important transition in the final verse of today's reading. Up to this Jesus had spoken in the past tense of the bread that had come down from heaven. Now he changes to the future tense ... 'the bread that I shall give is my flesh for the life of the world.'

With the psalmist we praise and bless, boast of and glorify the Lord whose flesh is given for life's journey to the holy mountain.

Taste and see that the Lord is good.

REVERE THE LORD
Psalm 32:2-3, 10-15

Jesus began to speak in the future tense: 'The bread that I shall give is my flesh for the life of the world.' He repeated the point in six different expressions, so there are seven statements developing the theme of the bread of life. Faith recognises the fulfilment of this promise in the sacred bread of the Eucharist.

The psalm of the day is the same as last Sunday except that some different verses are chosen. Certain lines of the psalm may be taken to highlight the reverence of mind and body due to the Blessed Sacrament.

Revere the Lord, you his saints.

The awesome privilege of receiving the Lord calls for profound reverence. This is no casual meeting but an encounter with Jesus deserving our utmost reverence and attention. The Eucharist is the Lord coming as the food of life ... 'whoever eats me draws life from me.' Catholics continue to reverence the presence of the Lord in the sacred hosts which have not been consumed. These are placed in the sacred tabernacle. We genuflect before the Lord here present and maintain a sanctuary light as a reminder of the divine presence. We receive the blessing of the Lord in Benediction of the Most Blessed Sacrament.

Keep your tongue from evil and your lips from speaking deceit.

The tongue which receives the sacred host and the lips which drink the chalice should never be sullied by words of profanity, deceit or hurt. Reverence grows in mind and heart and is manifested in outward action.

I will bless the Lord at all times.

DECISION TIME
Psalm 33:2-3, 16-23

John's discourse on the bread of life ends with a division of the ways: the unbelievers drift away while the believers stay. Simon Peter speaks on behalf of the believers: 'Lord, who shall we go to? You have the message of eternal life.' This may be the moment that Jesus referred to when he said at the last supper discourse: 'You are pruned already by means of the word that I have spoken to you' (Jn 15:3). It was also a time of decision for Joshua's people in the first reading.

Psalm 33 is used for the third successive Sunday. The verses selected for today also see an opposition of ways. The wicked (sinners) go one way, the just another.

The Lord turns his face against the wicked ...
The Lord turns his eyes to the just
and his ears to their appeal.

The lot of believers is not necessarily an easy path. The psalm speaks of distress, being broken-hearted, crushed in spirit, suffering many trials. But they are assured that the Lord sees and hears. It is similar to the beatitudes which declare the blessing of God on the poor in spirit, the gentle, the oppressed and persecuted. But their consolations are all promised in the future tense.

The Lord turns his face to us in a very special way by the gift of the Eucharist. Faith tells us that the Lord is our companion through his body given up for us and his blood shed in the new covenant. Companion literally means one who shares bread with me.

Taste and see that the Lord is good.

INNER INTEGRITY
Psalm 14:2-5

As pilgrims enter the temple of the Lord they have an examination of conscience, just as we have at the start of Mass. *Lord, who shall dwell on your holy mountain?* The voice of the priest is then heard with a list of qualities which we can consider under the headings of justice, reverence and integrity.

Justice is to be the guideline of our actions. It involves speaking the truth from the heart, wronging nobody and not casting a slur on our neighbour.

Reverence, in the sense of valuing the gift of faith, is protected by one *who holds the godless in disdain, but honours those who fear the Lord.* That means avoiding the people or situations which would weaken our faith, while seeking those situations or people which strengthen our relationship with God.

Integrity ensures that one is faithful to one's state of life in marriage or religious commitment, *come what may.* It means never availing of the chance to take the rip off somebody ... *takes no interest on a loan.* Nor does one accept bribes.

Moral instruction may be given in such guidelines but moral strength comes from within. *Such a one will stand firm forever.* It seems that the religious teachers of Jesus' day got so caught up in the minutiae of external observance that they lost sight of the inner heart. Jesus saw the bigger picture and reminded them that it is from the heart that evil intentions emerge. His list of evil deeds reads like the back cover of a best-selling novel!

The just will live in the presence of the Lord.

PRAISE THE LORD
Psalm 145:7-10

Today's readings celebrate healing. In Mark's gospel, an individual is sometimes taken to represent the group. The deaf man with the impediment of speech represents the pagan people of 'Galilee of the gentiles'. Jesus opened their ears to hear his word and loosened their tongues to proclaim his message. These actions may be recalled in the ceremony of baptism.

The psalm of the day praises God for all works of justice and healing. *My soul, give praise to the Lord.* When Francis of Assisi saw something beautiful, he was moved to praise the artist of that beauty. Our psalm today is an invitation to see the good deeds of people and to praise God whose grace is to be seen in this goodness.

Miraculous healings are rare and the vast majority of healing actions are performed through medical skill and devoted care. But it is the Lord who first bestowed these human talents. Similarly, divine intervention in matters of justice happens through people who work for justice. The psalm repeatedly recognises the Lord's part: *It is the Lord.* It reminds one of the beloved disciple's recognition of the Risen Lord after the huge catch of fish.

It is the Lord whose grace motivates people to work for justice, to feed the hungry, to minister to the sick, to teach the blind, to welcome the stranger, to care for the poor.

May our eyes be opened to see their goodness and may our tongues be loosened to praise the Lord, the giver of all goodness.

My soul, give praise to the Lord.

A FOLLOWER OF MINE
Psalm 114:1-6, 8-9

Jesus asked the question of his disciples, 'Who do you say that I am?' Let us suppose that they in turn asked Jesus, 'Well, what have you to say for yourself. Who do you say that you are?' Might he not have answered like this: 'I am come to deliver you beyond the limitations of suffering, even of death itself. I am to do this by taking on all that evil can throw at me. But by going into death I will open up the way to resurrected life.'

The culminating event of salvation history occurred in the death and resurrection of Jesus Christ. Saint Paul more than anybody else explained the symbolism of the water of baptism as our entry into the pattern of dying and rising with Christ. Everything we suffer or struggle with is sharing in the cross of Christ: and every experience of grace is sharing in the resurrection.

The triumph of Jesus Christ was a fulfilment of the extraordinary hope expressed in the Servant Songs of Deutero-Isaiah, one of which provides today's first reading.

The accompanying psalm is a prayer of thanksgiving to God for safe deliverance from *the snares of death ... the anguish of the tomb ... sorrow and distress.* Renewed in strength, the psalmist rejoices with that appreciation of life which belongs to those who have been close to death.

I will walk in the presence of the Lord,
in the land of the living.

It is the privilege of the baptised to walk each day in the footsteps of Christ's death and resurrection.

FACING OPPOSITION
Psalm 53:3-6, 8

The psalms are a great school of honest prayer, responding to God out of real life situations. The psalmist does not hide his feelings behind a veil of piosity. If he is angry with God, he says so. If he has a problem with somebody, he says so. Here is an example of how to pray when people are out to get you.

The proud have risen against me,
ruthless men seek my life.

The troublemakers are said to have no regard for God. But the psalmist responds in confidence: *I have God for my help.* He appeals to the name of God to save him, and to the power of God to uphold his cause.

Anybody who is unjustly opposed or accused is in good company for it happened to Jesus and to the writer of Wisdom. Anybody who stands up for a moral ideal sets off a negative reaction in others. The eye is made for light but light hurts the sore eye. Similarly, goodness is a reproach to the sick soul. The shape of the cross captures Jesus, the innocent victim, at the centre of negative energies coming in from all four quarters.

It is important not to let the wrongs of others set up a negative agenda in your life. Our psalm turns from the wrongs of others to the praise of God. As another psalm puts it:

I have found praise to foil the enemy, to silence the foe and the rebel.

DISCERNMENT
Psalm 18:8, 10, 12-14

Today's psalm raises some very pertinent questions in the area of discernment.

- How can I detect all my errors?
- What are my hidden faults? Perhaps others can see them but I can't.
- Does presumption rule me? I have met self-appointed prophets presuming divine inspiration behind their messages for me. But am I also guilty of presuming that my opinion is of God's direction?

The issue of discernment arises in today's first reading and gospel. Moses and Jesus decide that if good is being done then the matter is of God's direction. By their fruits you shall know them.

The writer of Psalm 18 seeks his guidance from God's revelation, first in the grandeur of creation and then in what is called the law.

The heavens proclaim the glory of God
and the firmament shows forth the work of his hands.

The law of the Lord is an all-embracing term for the covenanted relationship of God and his people, including their beliefs, moral code and directions for cultic celebrations. *The law of the Lord is perfect ... revives the soul ... gives wisdom to the simple ... gladdens the heart ... gives light to the eyes.*

Counselling can help me to sort out the layers of my experiences to enable me to see where I am and what I need to do. The task of spiritual direction is to see where God is involved in all this.

The rule of the Lord is to be trusted,
it gives wisdom to the simple.

OF MARRIAGE AND CHILDREN
Psalm 127

It is significant that the teaching of the Lord on the inviolability of the sacred bond of marriage is followed immediately by the story of welcoming the children with warmth and blessing. The people who suffer most in the break-up of marriage are the children. Parents owe their children fidelity and stability as the foundation of psychological maturity. Are we going to see the day when offspring will sue their parents for dereliction of responsibility?

The responsorial psalm pictures the ideal family of that day: God-fearing, labouring, happy, prospering and spreading out from the central table. These were different times when life expectancy was much shorter, less attention was paid to interpersonal relationships and the workplace was closely related to the home. Yet the values reflected in the psalm remain valid, especially the value that is inherent in the last line: *On Israel, peace!* The peace and stability of a nation is dependent on the quality of family life.

It comes as no surprise that studies show that the children who suffered from broken relationships were more prone to anxiety, depression, crime, drug and alcohol abuse, inability to trust or stay in a job etc. The list of harmful results is endless.

Winston Churchill's famous saying about democracy is applicable to marriage. It is the worst system that we have, apart from the alternatives. To work at marriage involves an investment of time, generosity, trust, fidelity, sacrifice, caring and compassion. With the psalmist we pray:

May the Lord bless us all the days of our life.

THE BIGGER PICTURE
Psalm 89:12-17

Mark describes Jesus setting out on a journey. Journeys are important in Mark's gospel. Discipleship is an invitation to follow Jesus in his journey to Jerusalem. Is this rich man who approaches Jesus ready to walk with him? Jesus looked at him with love. But because of his attachment to his wealth, he went away ... on another road ... sad. Notice how his face fell, all inner energy disintegrating. What a contrast with the loving invitation of Jesus!

What was this man lacking? The writer of the first reading would call it wisdom: the bigger picture: seeing everything from God's panoramic point of view.

I confess to being very keen on sport. I prefer being at a game than watching it on television. One misses the close-up shots and the action replays, but at the game one is more aware of the off the ball movement, the personal duels and the electricity in the air. Again, it's the bigger picture, the more complete story.

The psalmist prays: *Make us know the shortness of our life that we may gain wisdom of heart.* Would the rich, young man have acted differently if he had pondered on that line. 'Compared to her (wisdom), I held riches as nothing ... all gold is a pinch of sand.'

Wisdom knows that our dark times (when God seems angry) will change to morning when we are filled with God's love. The psalm prays for *joy to balance our affliction, for the years when we knew misfortune.*

Let the favour of the Lord be upon us.

OUR AMBITIONS AND HOPES
Psalm 32:4-5, 8-20, 22

Coming up to Christmas I like asking children what do they hope to get from Santa. Some children will immediately reel off a list of what they want to get. Others simply answer, 'a surprise.' I like to think that the latter answer is the expression of total trust in the love and judgement of the child's parents.

James and John were more like the first category of children. They knew clearly what they wanted: top seats in the house. Personal ambition, regardless of others, was their driving force. Not that the other apostles were any better: indignant, they were. Jesus called them to a conversion of ways: from the ambition to get to the ambition to give. Greatness is in the giving rather than in the receiving.

The first reading is about one who is known as the suffering servant of God. Even when he is crushed by suffering he still trusts that God will vindicate his cause. He is willing to offer his life in atonement so that others may be justified when they see the good outcome in God's time. Greatness is in the serving.

The psalm picks up his total trust ... *we place all our hope in you*. The psalmist and the suffering servant resemble the second sort of child, totally trusting in the parents' love. God's word is faithful and his works to be trusted ... *our soul is waiting for the Lord* ... for a surprise!

May your love be upon us, O Lord,
as we place all our hope in you.

DELIVERANCE
Psalm 125

Picking up the celebration of the return of the exiled Jews to their native land, this short psalm celebrates deliverance from bondage in Babylon. *It seemed like a dream*, almost too good to be true.

Then was our mouth filled with laughter,
on our lips there were songs.

The story of God's redeeming love is a marvel to be celebrated every day. But, sadly, we too easily pass through this world blind to its wonders. With Bartimaeus we cry out that we might see.

Helen Keller, physically blind and deaf, once asked a friend if she had seen anything interesting while walking in the forest. 'Nothing, really.' Helen, who could catch the singing of a bird on a branch through vibrations, was stunned. Which of the two was the more blind?

There are many ways that we walk in darkness: prejudice, obstinacy, refusal to accept another point of view, seeing only the faults of others and never their virtues or successes. Blind to the traces of God's artistry in the beauty and grandeur of the world. If I pass a day without responding in praise to God, I should ask myself what holds me in bondage. When Bartimaeus was released from his prison of darkness, he threw off his cloak like he would chains, jumped up and followed Jesus along the way.

Master, let me see again.
Deliver us, O Lord, from our bondage.
May our eyes be opened to your wonders.
And our ears receptive to your story.
What marvels the Lord worked for us,
Indeed we were glad.

LOVING WITH STRENGTH
Psalm 17:2-4, 47, 51

The responsorial verses we have today are selected from a long psalm, attributed to King David, thanking God for granting him victory and deliverance in countless battles. The names that David gives to God reflect the fighter's world ... *my strength, my rock, my fortress, my saviour, my shield, my mighty help.* Yet, for all these hard images, there is a tenderness in the opening line: *I love you, Lord, my strength.* Perhaps a key to the whole psalm is a line which is not in today's selected verses: *The Lord saved me because he loved me.*

Later in the psalm there are fairly gory details of how David pursued his foes and smote them so that they could not rise. Giving David the benefit of a charitable interpretation, we might say that this zealous smiting of foes was performed in the service of God and in the defence of faith and justice. In such a light, David's battles were his way of loving God with all his strength.

The text about loving God with all our faculties, known as the *Shemah,* was to be worn by every Jew, either in a wristband or headband (phylactery). Despite his faults, David is seen to have been a person who loved God ...

 – with a heart responding to God's love,

 – a mind ever searching for God,

 – a soul thirsting for God's eternal beauty,

 – and with all his strength serving God amid waves of death and torrents of destruction

I love you, Lord, my strength.

TOTAL GIVING
Psalm 145:7-10

This psalm is one of the *hallel*, that is *alleluia*, psalms, to be sung in praise of God. God is praised for being faithful and trustworthy, in contrast to the princes and people of this world who can let you down. God's faithful love comes through to people in downtrodden circumstances ... the oppressed, the hungry, prisoners, blind, bowed down, the stranger ... and *the Lord upholds the widow and orphan.*

The first reading and gospel each highlight the heroic generosity of a widow. Mark has the habit of following some teaching of the Lord with the example of a person who embodies that lesson. Last Sunday we had the most important law of any religion, to love the Lord with all one's heart, mind, soul and strength. Jesus called the attention of the disciples to the poor widow who put into the collection box everything she possessed, all she had to live on. She is a model of discipleship as well as anticipating the total self-giving of Jesus which was to take place shortly afterwards.

There is a contrast between the showy, hypocritical religion of some of the scribes and the humble, unobtrusive dedication of the widow. God looks at the inner heart and is not deluded by outward show. There are no calculators in heaven, only the scales of love. A simple act of love is of more value than massive schemes without love. God, who sees all that is done in secret, will not be stinting in reward.

My soul, give praise to the Lord.

MY PORTION AND CUP
Psalm 15:5, 8-11

November's liturgy would not be complete without readings about the end-times. The psalm of the day was chosen for the verse:

For you will not leave my soul among the dead,
nor let your beloved know decay.

Belief in a meaningful life after death was not clear in the Old Testament until the last two hundred years before Christ. Today's reading from Daniel expresses this clearly developed belief in afterlife and the separation of the just from the shamed ... 'some to everlasting life, some to shame and disgrace.' The psalms date from a much earlier period. When the psalmist thanked God for not leaving his soul among the dead he was referring to deliverance from a close shave with death. However, this did not stop the early Christians from taking these lines as a foretelling of the resurrection of Jesus from the dead. We find this interpretation in the preaching of Peter and Paul in Acts. This is an instance of the fuller sense of scripture, when one text acquires a new level of meaning when seen in a larger context. As Thomas Merton put it, the psalms were like the water at Cana, waiting for Jesus to turn them into wine.

November's preaching should never be doleful or terrifying. The sadness of death gives way to the bright promise of immortality. We are happy to call the Lord *my portion and cup ... my prize.*

You will show me the path of life,
the fullness of joy in your presence,
at your right hand happiness for ever.

THE LORD IS KING
Psalm 92:1-2, 5

The last Sunday of the liturgical year is a suitable time to celebrate the kingship of Christ for two reasons. Firstly, the end of the year anticipates the end of time, when 'the Kingdom of God will come in its fullness. Then the just will reign with Christ for ever, glorified in body and soul, and the material universe itself will be transformed. God will be "all in all", in eternal life' (*Catechism*, 1060).

Secondly, the final Sunday reaches the climax of the gospels' gradual unveiling of the priesthood and kingship of Jesus. 'You anointed Jesus Christ, your only Son, with the oil of gladness, as the eternal priest and universal king' (Preface). In the course of his public ministry Jesus shunned any identification with earthly kingship but, in the final exchange with Pilate, he accepts that he is a king, though not of this world.

Recognising the divinity and universal kingship of Jesus, we apply to him the psalm which is about God's majesty. Being one with the Father, he is enrobed in majesty, might and power.

The world you made firm, not to be moved;
your throne has stood firm from of old.
From all eternity, O Lord, you are.

Jesus is the Alpha and the Omega, who is, who was, and who is to come, the Almighty.

His *decrees are to be trusted*, for they lead to 'a kingdom of truth and life, a kingdom of holiness and grace, a kingdom of justice, love and peace' (Preface).

The Lord is king, with majesty enrobed.

STAND ERECT
Psalm 24:4-5, 8-9, 10, 14

Our usual idea of time is sequential: we move forward ever more distant from the starting point. Liturgical time is circular as it ends in the beginning and begins at the end. God is the beginning and the end. From meditating on the past we draw direction and hope for the future. Celebrating the advent of God draws together dimensions of past history, future hope and present alertness.

The First Sunday of Advent every year draws attention to the future coming of the Lord at the end of time. The evangelists speak of the end-time in apocalyptic terms which arouse feelings of fear and distress but also of hope and expectation. 'Stand erect, hold your heads high, because your liberation is near at hand.'

The verses of the psalm chosen for today express an alert attentiveness to God. *To you, O Lord, I lift up my soul.* The classical definition of prayer is the raising of the heart and mind to God. Prayerfulness is the art of being constantly attentive to God. With the psalmist we offer our minds to God that he might teach us to walk in his ways and know his truth. Nobody has gone so far astray as to be beyond his saving mercy. *He shows the path to those who stray.*

The spiritual message of Advent has been submerged under the tide of a commercial Christmas. As Luke warned, hearts are coarsened with debauchery, drunkenness and the cares of life.

Maranatha, come Lord Jesus, to you I lift up my soul.

DARING TO DREAM
Psalm 125

Here is a psalm which obviously celebrates the release of the exiles from their bondage in Babylon. *It seemed like a dream ...* almost too good to be true. The psalmist attributes the good news to God. *What marvels the Lord worked for us! Indeed we were glad.*

The story of what God did in the past gives us hope in our troubles today. Advent brings a spirituality of hope into the darkness of winter. Hope is a virtue that enables one to dare to dream. Preparing for the feast of the incarnation reaffirms our belief in the coming of God. Yes, God does get involved in human affairs. Our church may be experiencing a winter in the darkness of scandals, falling numbers and rampant licentiousness in society. But we are a people of hope. *Deliver us, O Lord, from our bondage as streams in dry land.*

Advent helps us get in touch with the wilderness in ourselves, in society and in the church. It may be painful ... but it was in the wilderness that the word of God came to John. The Lord compared the word to a seed, a dynamic symbol of hope.

Those who are sowing in tears will sing when they reap.

Let's not get caught up in the rush to Christmas but allow time to the spirituality of Advent. Advent gets us in touch with winter and wilderness but it offers hope in the coming of God. Hope is the courage to dream.

Those who are sowing in tears
will sing when they reap.

THE WELLS OF SALVATION
Isaiah 12:2-6

The nearness or presence of God in our midst is the focus of today's liturgy. The prophet Zephaniah introduces the theme. The Assyrian invaders had devastated the northern kingdom and appeared ready to do the same to Jerusalem. However, they withdrew their armies. Zephaniah attributed the rescue to God. 'The Lord your God is in your midst, a victorious warrior.'

His words are repeated in the song of Isaiah which is used for today's psalm: *For great in your midst is the Holy One of Israel.* He writes of God as *my salvation ... my strength, my song.* He introduces an intriguing image of hope.

With joy you will draw water
from the wells of salvation.

Before the availability of piped water on tap, people had to let down their buckets and draw up water from a well. It pictures the deep, inner resource that one needs to draw from at a time of spiritual need.

Paul was caged up in prison when he was writing to the Philippians. Being a driven, active man, he would have been in spiritual turmoil if he had not possessed a deep inner well of faith. But from his conviction that the Lord is near he drew a great happiness which he wants to share with the Philippians. He urges them to show this inner happiness in two ways: tolerance towards others and a trust in God which banishes worry.

Will the good news of Christmas make me more patient and tolerant? Less worried? Truly happy?

With joy you will draw water
from the wells of salvation.

SHEPHERD OF ISRAEL
Psalm 79:2-3, 15-16, 18-19

The prophet Micah condemned the social injustice and wide-spread corruption of his day, but he offered hope that, in God's time, a leader would appear to shepherd the people towards true peace. Ephrathah was one of the smallest clans of Juda. In their territory lay Bethlehem, a tiny village. But unimportant Bethlehem could lay claim to being the birthplace of David, the shepherd boy chosen to be king. A return to the golden days of David's reign became one of the great hopes of Israel. The hope of Micah concerns the birth of this Davidic ruler, one who will feed his flock with the power of God.

The verses of the psalm carry on this hope for the messianic ruler, the true shepherd in the likeness of David. There is bold-ness and urgency in the prayer to *bring us back ... hear us ... shine forth ... rouse up your might ... come to our help ... look down from heaven and see ... visit this vine.*

In the fullness of time, the face of God shone on a young mother-to-be who traversed the hills of Juda to visit her cousin Elizabeth. Filled by the Holy Spirit, Elizabeth responded in words of wonder: 'Why should I be honoured with a visit from the mother of my Lord?'

Ephrathah was an insignificant clan, Bethlehem a tiny village and Mary, dedicated to virginity, a most unlikely mother. Should we be surprised at the presence of God in a tiny baby?

Let your face shine on us and we shall be saved.

Reflections for Christmas Day, Second Sunday of Christmas and Feast of the Epiphany are to be found in Cycle A.

TEMPLE OF LOVE
Psalm 83:2-3, 5-6, 9-10

My reflection on this psalm was interrupted by Michael. Rather, it received a new direction from Michael. He rang the doorbell, wanting to talk with a priest. Twenty-six, no longer wanted by his partner who is the mother of his sixteen-month old baby. He went back to his mother who told him to get lost. It is understandable that he feels he cannot relate to others in love, that he cannot sustain a relationship. He wants to believe in God. Is there any hope of things getting better? He showed me another side of family life.

Our psalm is about that lovely house where God dwells. It is the song of pilgrims on the way to the temple. One verse, not recited today, is about going through the Bitter Valley.

As they go through the Bitter Valley
they make it a place of springs.

This refers not to any particular place but to the pilgrims' experience of tiredness and thirst. Their desire to reach God's house transcends all hardship.

In prayer on the feast of family life, we remember all those have never known family love and security. Their Bitter Valley appears to have no way out. As Michael asked me, is there any chance that things might get better?

O Lord, hear my prayer, give ear, O God of Jacob
Turn your eyes, O God, our shield,
Look on the face of your anointed.

Where there is love, there God lives among people. May all rejected people and all who had a lonely Christmas find that temple of love and acceptance.

BAPTISED UNTO MISSION
Psalm 103:1-2, 3-4, 24-25, 27-30

The full celebration of the Epiphany, or manifestation of the divinity of Christ, involves the visit of the Magi, the voice of the Father at the baptism in the Jordan and the first miracle of Jesus (next Sunday's gospel).

The psalm chosen for today is a beautiful canticle of the revelation of God's power and grandeur in creation. One of Shakespeare's characters rhapsodised about tongues in stones, books in the running brooks, sermons in stones and good in everything. To the observant soul everything is a sacred word from above.

The psalm pictures the palace of the Creator up above the rain-clouds. The fluffy, white clouds that scud across the sky are the chariot of God. God walks on the wings of the wind, bearing his message afar. Fire, the gift from heaven, is his servant. All creatures of land and sea look to God for their food in due season.

The secret of creation is the breath of God. Genesis describes God saying things into life. When God sends forth his spirit or breath, things spring into life. Breath is life on loan from God. To die is to return this breath or spirit to God.

At the baptism of Jesus, the Holy Spirit descended on him, marking the beginning of his public ministry. At his death on Calvary, his mission accomplished, his last breath is the return of life to the Father. Then on the first day of Easter the risen Lord breathed the Spirit on the disciples and inaugurated their mission. To be baptised means sharing in that mission.

You send forth your spirit, they are created.

ANGELS OF PROTECTION
Psalm 90:1-2, 10-15

Here is a classical prayer of trust in God for protection all through the journey of life.

For you has he commanded his angels,
to keep you in all your ways.

The psalm is used in today's liturgy as a response to the reading from Deuteronomy, which is the closest we get to a Creed in the Old Testament. It is a declaration of belief that God had chosen, rescued and protected this people on all their ways.

The devil quoted the lines about the angels of protection in tempting Jesus. His answer made the distinction between trusting God and testing God, which is the reaction of one who doubts rather than trusts.

This psalm has been chosen as the ideal night prayer in the breviary. The darkness of night holds no fear for those *who dwell in the shelter of the Most High and abide in the shade of the Almighty.* Such is the depth of trust expressed that the text of this psalm has often been used by people as a sacred talisman to protect them from harm. The novelist, Boris Pasternack, describes Doctor Zhivago finding portions of the psalm sewn into the garments of the soldiers he was treating.

Who are the angels sent to guard us? We may think of our personal Guardian Angels, or apply the idea to God's messengers who come in the form of caring people who help us over our bumpy roads or in our dark nights.

My refuge, my strength, my God in whom I trust.

THE FACE OF GOD
Psalm 26:1, 7-9, 13-14

The Second Sunday of Lent might be called Encouragement Sunday because of the gospel of the transfiguration. The life of faith is modelled on the story of Abraham. He was called to leave the security of home to travel on the strength of God's word, promising a rich land. 'How am I to know?', he asked. God's presence was made known to him in the form of fire.

Responding to this reading is a psalm of light. *The Lord is my light and my help.* It was in brilliant light that Jesus was transfigured on the mountain of prayer.

It is your face, O Lord, that I seek;
hide not your face.

The three apostles who would later see the face of Jesus sweating blood in agony were sustained by the memory of that face brilliant in divine light. They were told to listen to him.

Listen to the word and see the face. *Lectio Divina* involves staying with the words of scripture until we can see the face of God in our daily experiences: moving from the word then to the word now. Like smelting metal until the face of the purifier is reflected on the surface.

It sets us a positive challenge for Lent: to spend more time pondering the word; to let the sacred texts change my focus from the faults of others towards seeing how God is given a face in their graces and virtues. That is how *I shall see the Lord's goodness in the land of the living.*

It is your face, O Lord, that I seek, hide not your face.

A GOD OF COMPASSION
Psalm 102:1-4, 6-8, 11

The idea still persists in some quarters that when some accident or misfortune happens to somebody, it is to be understood as a punishment from God for some sin, either committed personally or by a family member, even in a past generation. The unfortunate victim is then left with fear of a tyrannical God, or a God 'who has it in for me'. After two local tragedies in Galilee, Jesus tried to move people on from that horrible idea of God. Instead of passing judgement on those who were killed, the only conscience we are to judge is our own. Then he added a parable of great encouragement, about the gardener who wants to give the fruitless tree one more chance. God is the one who so cares for us that he is always ready to give us one more chance.

There is no more appropriate psalm for this gospel than the one chosen for today. *The Lord is compassion and love.* It is one thing to say that God has compassion: it means more to say that God is compassion ... and love.

The psalmist asks his soul to *give thanks to the Lord and to bless his holy name. God forgives all your guilt ... heals every one of your ills ... redeems your life from the grave ... crowns you with love and compassion.* This compassionate God is the transcendent 'I Am who I Am' revealed to Moses in the first reading.

Lent's penance is a way of blessing God who is *slow to anger and rich in mercy.*

TASTE AND SEE
Psalm 33:2-7

Taste and see that the Lord is good.

This line is an appropriate response to the first reading's account of the first meal of the Israelites on the produce of the land of their destiny.

Meals are very significant in Luke's gospel. Nowadays we can hardly appreciate the deep significance of table-fellowship in biblical times. When a person had to grow most of their own food, to share table with somebody was an expression of sharing life. Hence the absolute shock of seeing Jesus eating with people regarded as sinners. The parable of the Prodigal Son reaches its climax in the contrast between the father who takes the wayward son back to the table and the elder son who refuses to do so.

The psalm of the day might be heard on the lips of the forgiven prodigal. The banquet for his return was rendered all the more tasteful by the father's goodness. This father figure gives a human face to the mercy of God. Picture the relief and joy on the son's face, reflecting the radiance of the father at the head of the table.

Look towards him and be radiant;
let your faces not be abashed.

The prodigal recalls the doubts and anxieties he had experienced before he was embraced in the father's forgiveness. He makes his own the lines of the psalm:

This poor man called; the Lord heard him
and rescued him from all his distress.

The radiant face of the Father invites us to an honest confession this Lent.

Taste and see that the Lord is good.

DELIVERANCE FROM BONDAGE
Psalm 125

Deliverance is one of the major themes of the psalms. Deliverance from slavery in Egypt, and later from forced exile in Babylon, were the two strongest supporting pillars of Jewish memory. Their God was a God who saves. Isaiah, in our first reading, celebrates the end of the Babylonian bondage. 'No need to recall the past ... See I am doing a new deed.'

In the fullness of time, the promised one came and his name is Jesus, meaning one who saves. In today's second reading, Paul looks on everything else as rubbish in comparison with knowing Christ Jesus. The liberation, which Jesus was to win for all people, is anticipated in the story of one woman: saved from death by stoning and encouraged to sin no more.

Today's joyous psalm of deliverance originally celebrated liberation from Babylon, but it would lie just as comfortably on the lips of those who were freed from Egyptian slavery, or of Paul or the adulterous woman.

What marvels the Lord worked for us!

Indeed we were glad.

Lent advances and we are close to the annual celebration of the saving deeds of Jesus in his death and resurrection. We will appreciate what he has done for us only to the extent that we recognise the bondage of evil power from which he has liberated us. His grace works like *streams in dry land*. Whatever penance we are doing for Lent is co-operating with his saving death.

Those who are sowing in tears

will sing when they reap.

The reflections for Palm Sunday and Easter Sunday may be found in Cycle A.

LOVE HAS NO END
Psalm 117:2-4, 22-27

The sons of Israel were the whole nation of believers. *The sons of Aaron* were the clergy of the day. *Those who fear the Lord* were those from outside the Jewish nation who had come to share their faith in God. All are called to proclaim that his love has no end. Saint Paul told the Corinthians that there are three things that last: faith, hope and love; and the greatest of these is love.

It seemed, in the darkness of Calvary, that evil had silenced the good news, that hatred had choked the life out of love, and that death had claimed the ultimate prize. All of us have experienced moments of Calvary darkness and feelings of rejection. Then, through closed doors, into the room of fear, comes the Risen Lord, our Saviour. He shows the wounds of rejection but his greeting is full of peace and his very breath bestows the Spirit of forgiveness and divine love.

The stone which the builders rejected has become the corner stone. The disciples are bonded into a living community of praying, caring and sharing. The power of the Lord is seen in miracles of healing. The Holy Spirit becomes the breath of energy in the mission of the church. Thomas, who had refused to believe, makes the highest act of faith of anybody in the New Testament.

Love goes beyond death, for love has no end.

Forgiveness goes beyond sin, for love has no end.

Give thanks to the Lord, for his love has no end.

DYING AND RISING
Psalm 29:2, 4-6, 11-13

O Lord, you have raised my soul from the dead,
restored me to life from those who sink into the grave.

The psalms were composed before people had developed any clear belief in a meaningful life after death. What the psalmist is celebrating is an escape from death-threatening experience ... which, in reality, was but the temporary postponement of inevitable death.

I will praise you, Lord, you have rescued me.

Applying the psalm to Jesus Christ, what we celebrate is not an escape from death but a liberation through death. Jesus did not avoid death but saw it as the door out of this life into heavenly life. Lazarus and others were resuscitated: they came back to earthly life. Jesus was not resuscitated but, in resurrection, he went forward to the higher life.

It is said that those who die well are those who have died often. There is a little death every time we let go of something in order to move on to something else: when we voluntarily give up something good for the sake of an ideal; when we let go of personal grief to let somebody we love move on; when we resist temptation. These little experiences of dying are part of our baptismal union with the death and resurrection of the Lord. In today's gospel Jesus speaks of the way Peter would let go of his impetuosity in preparation for the death by which he would give glory to God.

Belief that we are called to share in the resurrection changes everything. *You have changed my mourning into dancing.*

CALLED TO SERVE
Psalm 99:1-3, 5

On this Sunday each year, the gospel is about Jesus as shepherd. This suits the designation of the day as Vocations Sunday. 'The sheep that belong to me listen to my voice; I know them and they follow me.' It is a day for praying that the church will not lack people who answer the call of the Lord to dedicate their lives in God's service.

With a stretch of the imagination, we can detect in the responsorial psalm some of the forms of ministry or service to which people are called by the Lord. The psalm commences with the invitation to *all the earth* to *cry out with joy to the Lord.* Today's reading from Acts recounts the beginning of the mission to bring the good news to all nations, initiated by Paul and Barnabbas. The good news of salvation in Christ Jesus is a source of light and joy to people searching for meaning, for forgiveness and for life beyond the grave. 'I give them eternal life', said the Lord.

Down the ages the world has been enriched by those who answered the call to *serve the Lord with gladness.* The church has an unrivalled record in caring for the poor long before social services were available, and of educating and nursing long before the state took up these programmes.

The vocation to teach is a noble calling ... to remind people that *the Lord is God, he made us, we belong to him.*

He is faithful from age to age ... may those he has called be faithful also.

A COMMUNITY OF LOVE
Psalm 144:8-13

The three readings in today's liturgy have one theme in common: suffering is temporal and the glory is eternal. Paul and
Barnabas put new heart into the disciples with the message that
we have to experience many hardships before we enter the kingdom of God. Then the writer of the Apocalypse, after all the persecutions and tribulations of earlier chapters, describes his vision
of the new Jerusalem, where God lives among people. In the
extract from John's gospel, immediately after Judas had gone
out, as the passion was about to commence, Jesus spoke of his
glorification. He speaks of going away but he leaves a new com-
mandment: 'Love one another; just as I have loved you, you also
must love one another.' In John's theology, the new life of heaven
begins in a community of love on earth. As Cardinal Newman
put it: 'Grace in this life is glory in exile and glory is grace at
home.'

'Love ... as I have loved you.' In the responsorial psalm we
can find some of the qualities of Christian love.

The Lord is kind and full of compassion. The grace of the Lord's
presence in the apostolic community was manifest in their pool-
ing of resources and care for the poor.

Slow to anger and abounding in love. Christian love, after the
manner of Christ, does not return evil for evil, but remains a
positive river of energy that cleanses all pollutants. Christian
love will outlast any persecution and outlive all suffering

Yours is an everlasting kingdom;
your rule lasts from age to age.

FACES OF LIGHT
Psalm 66

O God, be gracious and bless us
and let your face shed its light upon us.

Surely one of the loveliest petitions ever composed! This psalm was originally used to praise God in anticipation of a good harvest. Rich fields and bountiful crops would reflect the smile of God on the people. As a psalm in Eastertide, we apply it to the abundant fruits of the resurrection. The Opening Prayer today asks God to help us celebrate our joy in the resurrection of the Lord and to express in our lives the love we celebrate.

Today's gospel sparkles with reasons for joy in our believing: being loved by the Father, God dwelling within us, the Holy Spirit teaching us, the gift of Christ's peace, the anticipation of the Lord returning to take us with him into glory. On the eve of the passion, Jesus could speak of peace. His peace is an inner strength drawn from union with the Father.

The wonder of the divine indwelling must be one of the world's best kept secrets. It is good news for all people. The repeated refrain is a prayer for all nations.

Let the people praise you, O God;
let all the peoples praise you.

Nice words are empty unless they are backed up by the witness of life. If the smile of God's love is reflected in the lives of Christians, then *will your name be known upon earth, and all nations learn your saving help.*

O God, be gracious and bless us
and let your face shed its light upon us.

CALLED TO GLORY
Psalm 96:1-2, 6-7, 9

This Sunday occurs during the great novena of prayer between the ascension and Pentecost. The liturgy of this in-between period continues to celebrate the ascension as well as looking expectantly towards Pentecost.

The psalm was for the enthronement of a king. It supplies us with the language of prayer to celebrate the glory of the risen, victorious Lord.

The Lord is king ... as Paul put it, Jesus has triumphed over all his enemies, and the last one to be destroyed was death.

Let earth rejoice, the many coastlands be glad ... the power of the Holy Spirit would send out the disciples to bring the news of Jesus to all nations.

His throne is justice and right ... as Jesus was vindicated in his glorification, so will the faithful be vindicated by sharing in his glory. Today's reading from the Apocalypse is about the vindication of those who proved faithful in all the trials and persecutions of the writer's day.

The skies proclaim his justice, all peoples see his glory ... at the martyrdom of Stephen, the heavens opened wide and there he saw the glory of God, and Jesus standing at God's right hand. The priestly prayer of Jesus is an intercession on our behalf: 'Father, I want those you have given me to be with me where I am, so that they may always see the glory you have given me.'

Jesus alone is Lord, *far above all spirits,* above any ideologies or idols that might be worshipped. May the Holy Spirit raise us up to be worthy of our calling.

The Reflections for the Ascension and Pentecost may be found in Cycle A.

THE WONDERS OF CREATION
Psalm 8:2, 4-9

The first reading, from Proverbs, offers a charming picture of God's creativity, playfulness and delight in being with his people. The God we believe in is not an abstract philosophical concept, nor a scientific remote control, but a family of intimate relationships, going forth and returning, creating, playing and drawing delight. Dame Julian of Norwich prayed to God as 'my maker, my lover and my upholder'.

How great is your name, O Lord our God,
through all the earth!

The psalmist contemplates the sky at night and is filled with a double wonder: wonder at the fantastic distances and complex laws that govern the movements of moon and stars; yet the great Creator has a personal care for each individual person.

What is man that you should keep him in mind,
mortal man that you care for him?

Human beings are made *little less than a god,* crowned with glory and honour, and put in charge of all the works of the Lord.

The growth of science has given us the technology to understand much more than the psalmist about the extent of the universe and the complex harmony of motions among the celestial bodies. Discoveries in astronomy or any branch of science ought not dispense with faith but should increase our sense of awe before the wonders of creation.

This psalm reminds us of God's personal care for all the works of his hand. It challenges us to respect every creature as a precious heritage put under our care by God.

BREAD AND WINE
Psalm 109:1-4

This is a psalm for the coronation of a king. A prophet speaks in God's name to the king, *sit on my right,* since the royal palace was to the right of God's temple in Jerusalem. Victory over his enemies is promised. Then the new king is reminded of his priestly role as a mediator between God and the people. He is not a cultic priest like the descendants of Aaron, but a king-priest *like Melchizedek of old.*

Melchizedek, in the first reading, offered bread and wine before blessing Abraham. This offering, recalled in the First Eucharistic Prayer, prefigured what Jesus did at the last supper. In today's second reading, Paul writes of that supper. When Jesus took the bread, he said, 'This is my body, which is for you, do this as a memorial of me.' Then taking the cup, he said, 'This cup is the new covenant in my blood. Whenever you drink it, do this as a memorial of me.'

Bread is a symbol with many ways of connection. It is the most common food, the staff of life, 'fruit of the earth and work of human hands'. A companion literally means one who shares bread with you. The Lord chose it as the material mode of his presence among us as companion on the road, as food to sustain us, as sanctifier of the earth and human work.

Wine is a symbol of celebration and joy. But it also expresses suffering through the crushing of grapes. Jesus made it the sacrificial blood which ratified the new covenant.

'Do this as a memorial of me.'
You are a priest for ever,
a priest like Melchizedek of old.

A NEW SONG
Psalm 95:1-3, 7-10

The third epiphany episode is the first miracle of Jesus, at the wedding in Cana. This event of divine revelation is celebrated as the second Mystery of Light in the Rosary. The evangelist John refers to the miracles of Jesus as signs, thereby urging the reader to move beyond the actual happening to the divine power in Jesus. John's summary is that Jesus let his glory be seen. The real wedding in the story is the marriage of heaven and earth.

Isaiah's encouragement to the returned exiles anticipated the wedding of God and his people. Just as the bride takes on a new name, that of her husband, they would no longer be mocked as a forsaken or abandoned people, but they would be called 'My Delight' and 'The Wedded'.

No wedding celebration is complete without a song. The psalm chosen for these readings calls us to *sing a new song to the Lord.* At Cana the water for purification represented the old religion which was a time of preparation. This was changed into wine to celebrate the wedding.

The wedding of heaven and earth which Jesus effected is renewed every time we celebrate the Eucharist. Liturgy is always a new song to the Lord, just as any good song is a new experience every time it is sung. It is our privilege in liturgy to join with the angels and saints in divine worship. In holy reverence we tremble before his divine kingship. It is a song that never grows old, *a new song to the Lord.*

THE WISDOM OF THE LAW
Psalm 18:8-10, 15

If you join a club or society you accept the constitution or rules of that body. These rules give practical expression to the identity, vision and aims of the society. When the Hebrew people returned to Jerusalem after the exile they were dispirited by the enormity of the task facing them. The priest, Ezra, gathered them for a day's retreat, and he read for them the laws of the covenant that God had offered them. They rediscovered their identity, clarified their targets and revived their spirits.

Luke did his research and writing to show how well founded was the teaching that his patron had received. Jesus applied the old text from Isaiah to himself so that the people of Nazareth, who thought that they knew him, might learn his real identity and mission.

Psalm 18 is about the revelation of God firstly in the grandeur of nature ... *the heavens proclaim the glory of God* ... and then through what is called the law. The Jews were a practical people who knew their God through the rules of worship and moral laws rather than by philosophical reflection or the riddles posed by a sage. *The law of the Lord is perfect, it revives the soul ... it gives wisdom to the simple.*

Sometimes religious rules might outlive their purpose, but by and large they must be respected as expressing the practical, moral implications of who were are before God. Rules were not created in a vacuum but are the fruit of experience and wisdom.

Your words are spirit, Lord, and they are life.

PRAYER IN OLD AGE
Psalm 70:1-6, 15, 17

Jesus experienced rejection from his neighbours in Nazareth. When Jeremiah received the call of God he was warned of the opposition he would face. 'No prophet is ever accepted in his own country.'

The psalm chosen to accompany these readings is the prayer of an old man who is experiencing a lot of opposition. He describes himself as *old and grey-headed*, and he appeals to God who has supported him from birth to be his rock of refuge. He resembles Jeremiah in his belief that he was under God's protection even before birth. *From my mother's womb you have been my help.*

It is sad to see people in their declining years struggling to hope. The psychologist, Erik Erikson, maintained that the eighth and final crisis of human development is between despair and integrity. Integrity means oneness, the wisdom that comes from experiencing the unity of all things in the larger picture of life. It is marked by peace. It sees the sifting of the unimportant things from the frame.

Integrity has to withstand many opposing voices. Despair means that all falls apart. The dissenting voices may come from external sources like scandals in the church, media criticism, falling numbers, loss of high standing in society. Or the negative arrows may come from within ... from personal guilt, consciousness of failure, doubts, inability to accept declining health.

The old and grey-headed psalmist continued to call God *a rock where I can take refuge ... my stronghold*. Let us pray this psalm for all who are struggling in their old age.

It is you, O Lord, who are my hope.

ALL THINGS ARE POSSIBLE
Psalm 137:1-5, 7-8

This is a rare Sunday when the three readings touch the same theme: the call of God to mission. Isaiah, Paul and Simon Peter received the call of God, and each in his own way experienced personal unworthiness in the light of God's power and holiness. On seeing the huge catch of fish, Peter felt how far he was from Jesus because he was a sinful man. Paul called himself the least of the apostles, not even deserving the name of apostle. Isaiah, after hearing the angels sing of God's holiness, felt himself wretched, lost, a man of unclean lips.

If we rely entirely on our own resources then personal unworthiness will prevent us from doing anything. However, true humility recognises that with God's help all things are possible. It is a lesson that Paul took to heart when God assured him that our weakness serves to make more room for God's grace to work. 'My power is at its best in weakness.'

The psalm of the day thanks God for help in days of trouble

I thank you, Lord, with all my heart,

you have heard the words of my mouth.

The next two lines are a perfect link with Isaiah's vision of the heavenly liturgy.

Before the angels I will bless you.

I will adore before your holy temple.

One line in the last verse might well have been Peter's prayer.

You stretch out your hand and save me.

Keep our eyes fixed on Jesus and all things are possible. But focus on the storm and we start to sink.

On the day I called, you answered.

THE TWO WAYS
Psalm 1: 1-4, 6

If you want some new piece of technology to work smoothly, it is advisable to follow the manufacturer's instructions. The same holds true for the smooth running of society. At the risk of being simplistic and naïve, I suggest that our manufacturer's instructions are in the Commandments and other expressions of God's law.

We may well wonder why the editor of the Book of Psalms chose today's psalm to be first in the collection. Is it intended as a preface to the Book? It introduces a theme that is popular in the wisdom of the Old Testament: the choice of the two ways; the way of obeying God's law or going one's own way. This black and white contrast between the blessings of the good life and the cursed condition of self-seeking is also the theme of today's first reading and gospel.

Notice the progressive steps downward in one who first *follows* the wrong counsel, then *lingers in the way of sinners* and finally *sits in the company of scorners*. Scorners are those who know everything that is wrong with church, government, everybody ... bar themselves. By contrast, the wise person constantly asks what does God want of me in this instance ... pondering on and delighting in God's law.

The wise person is compared to the healthy, evergreen tree beside the flowing waters *that yields its fruit in due season*. The opposite life is like *winnowed chaff,* emptied of grain. The foundation of social stability and personal happiness lies in respect for God's law.

Happy the man who has placed his trust in the Lord.

TO FORGIVE IS DIVINE
Psalm 102:1-4, 8, 10, 12-13

Today's liturgy celebrates the compassion of God which removes our sins as far as the east is from the west. God's love is a positive energy that is greater than any negative force.

The Lord is compassion and love,
slow to anger and rich in mercy.

David, in the first reading, spared the life of Saul because he regarded the king as the Lord's anointed. But he had no such qualms about killing other enemies. The teaching of Jesus advocates forgiveness for everybody, not just the king. The ethic of loving every enemy, blessing the persecutor and turning the other cheek is a necessary consequence of accepting God as our Father. Sadly, it is an ideal which has been tried only too rarely. Christian love is to be a surge of positive energy that refuses to be diverted or polluted by the wrongdoing of others. In this way 'you will be children of the Most High, for he himself is kind to the ungrateful and the wicked'. We call that the unconditional love of God.

He does not treat us according to our sins
nor repay us according to our faults.

Rabbi Jonathan Sacks writes that the one word which can change the course of history is forgiveness. It breaks the cycle of hatred producing hatred. He identifies forgiveness as the most compelling testimony to human freedom. Pope John Paul II described forgiveness as a threshold that evil cannot cross. In the immortal words of Alexander Pope, 'to err is human, to forgive, divine.'

THE POWER OF THE TONGUE
Psalm 91:2-3, 13-16

The power of the tongue, for good or for evil, is a thread running through today's readings. 'The test of a man is in his conversation,' we read in Ecclesiasticus. 'Do not praise a man before he has spoken, since this is the test of men.' As an orchard is judged by the quality or its fruit, similarly a 'a man's words betray what he feels.' The gospel develops this comparison to the fruit trees. 'For a man's words flow out from what fills his heart.'

The Letter of James graphically outlines the power of the tongue for goodness or for evil. It is a flame which can set a whole forest ablaze. The same tongue which blesses the Lord may be used to curse somebody who is made in God's image.

The psalm of the day celebrates some noble uses of speech. *It is good to give thanks to the Lord.* And not only to God, for it is very important to express gratitude and appreciation to one another.

It is good to make music to your name, O Most High. But that same holy name is often spat out in profanity. Profanity has been called the crutch of the inarticulate.

It is with the tongue that *we proclaim your love in the morning and your truth in the watches of the night.*

The psalmist promises that the person of inner integrity will flourish like the palm-tree, the symbol of prayer, and persevere to old age like the mighty Cedar of Lebanon.

It is good to give thanks to the Lord.

STRONG AND FAITHFUL
Psalm 116

Today's psalm may be the shortest in the book but its outreach is wide enough to embrace all nations and peoples. The response to the psalm expresses the key message of today's readings, that the good news is a message for all nations.

Go out to the whole world
and proclaim the good news.

It is the perfect echo of the prayer of Solomon in the first reading, that the prayer of any foreigner in the temple would be favourably heard by God. In the gospel, Luke, coming from a gentile background, takes a special delight in having Jesus credit the gentile Roman centurion with faith greater than anything he had found in Israel.

The psalm calls on all nations to praise the Lord because *strong is his love for us; he is faithful for ever*. The Roman centurion is a good example of these two qualities: love that is strong and faith that is full.

Strong love will transcend barriers such as colour, religious affiliation, class or rank. The centurion cared deeply for one who was a servant, someone of inferior rank. He was a man who had won the respect of the Jewish elders. He knew the strength of authority behind a military order and he assumed that the healing word of Jesus would carry the same strength.

The centurion was faithful in the sense of being full of faith. He believed that the power of love in Jesus could heal at a distance. Jesus was astonished at his faith. His prayer is ours before Holy Communion: 'Lord I am not worthy.'

POWER TO RAISE UP
Psalm 29:2, 4-6, 11-13

The first reading and the gospel relate how the prayer of Elijah and the word of Jesus each brought back life to the dead son of a widow. The accompanying psalm was chosen for the lines,

O Lord, you have raised my soul from the dead,
restored me to life from those who sink into the grave.

The psalmist had not actually died, but he is thanking God for rescuing him from some close shave with death. In a verse not quoted today, the psalmist describes how everything was going along swimmingly until God hid his face and he was spun into confusion. But he cried out to God, his prayer was heard and light returned.

His anger lasts a moment; his favour through life.
At night there are tears, but joy comes with dawn.

In these readings God is revealed as one who raises up, restores life, and gives the power of recovery.

Every Recovery Programme builds on two foundations: the admission of personal powerlessness over a certain problem; and the recognition of a Higher Power who/which can aid recovery. The person of faith identifies the Higher Power as God.

If the great dark realm of death is not beyond God's uplifting power, then neither are the clouds of darkness we experience in this life. There is no fall so final that it is beyond the power of Jesus to enable one start again. And there is no such word as 'hopeless' for one who believes in Jesus Christ.

'Young man, I tell you to get up.'

THE JOY OF FORGIVENESS
Psalm 31:1-2, 5-7, 11

One of the most fulfilling experiences of a priest's life is sharing in the relief, peace and joy of somebody whose guilt has been lifted by the mercy of the Lord. Today's psalm is a beautiful celebration of that happiness.

Happy the one whose offence is forgiven
whose sin is remitted.
O happy the one to whom the Lord
imputes no guilt.

In a verse not quoted today, the psalmist relates what anguish of mind, soul and body he suffered as long as he kept his guilt locked up inside.

But now I have acknowledged my sins;
my guilt I did not hide.
And you, Lord, have forgiven
the guilt of my sin.

As Jesus once said, it is the truth that sets us free. Telling your story, letting the past out, is essential in any psychological therapy. As a door is both a way out and a way in, when we open up the door in humble and honest confession, it is to let the guilt out and to allow God's cleansing power in. The sinful woman loved much because she had been forgiven much.

Since commencing this reflection I have been summoned several times to the confessional. I heard about fifteen confessions, mostly routine acts of devotion. In two instances, however, the absolving of the burden of guilt brought tears of relief to the penitent. To both, I quoted from this psalm. They knew what the psalmist meant:

Happy the one whose offence is forgiven
whose sin is remitted.

A DRY, WEARY LAND
Psalm 62:2-6, 8-9

Viktor Frankl found that the horrors of Auschwitz were like a breeze which quenched a weak flame of faith but fanned a stronger faith into an unquenchable fire. Today's readings focus on the growth of prayer in times of suffering.

The gospel of the day leads up to the first prediction of the passion. It is typical of Luke that he sets Jesus alone at prayer in preparation for the announcement. The accompanying reading from Zechariah promises the outpouring of a spirit of kindness and prayer. The prophet links it with people looking in mourning at the one they have pierced. John applied those words to the scene on Calvary.

Psalm 62, surely one of the most beautiful prayers ever composed, gives us the language of prayer in times of darkness, dryness and suffering. It speaks of longing, thirsting and pining for God, *like a dry, weary land without water.* Dry land we can imagine. But what is a weary land? Overused, no balanced rotation of crops, no fertilisers added. Like a person too busy, lacking balance of energies, without enrichment or input.

Our Catechism reads: 'Prayer is the encounter of God's thirst with ours. God thirsts that we might thirst for him.' Making time for prayer is the first requisite. Empty time to provide space for God. Dry time to purify the heart of self-seeking. Weary time to humble our self-sufficiency. Only in these times of desert experience can we really learn how to thirst for God, to pine for his consolations, to gaze in the sanctuary.

For you my soul is thirsting.

MY PORTION, MY CUP, MY PRIZE
Psalm 15:1-2, 5, 7-11

Legend has it that Luke was a portrait-painter. Certainly he gives us a vivid portrait of the face of Jesus resolutely set towards Jerusalem, the city of his destiny. Three would-be followers are challenged about the depth of their commitment. Elisha burned his plough and feasted on his oxen to show that there would be no turning back in his following of Elijah.

We turn to the responsorial psalm for an appropriate prayer of total trust and commitment. *Preserve me, God, I take refuge in you,* a way of saying that it is in you alone, Lord, that I trust. The psalm calls God *my portion, my cup, my prize.* When the Promised Land was portioned out to the twelve tribes, the tribe of Levi got no land because they were the priestly clan to whom God promised, 'It is I who will be your portion and inheritance' (Num 18:20). *My cup* expresses what one thirsts for. The image of my prize suggests the ambition, dedication and sacrifices made by the sportsperson in pursuit of victory.

The psalmist sets his heart on listening to the counsels of God, even in his dreams at night. He sets his eyes on the Lord, his daily support. The ultimate prize is life beyond death.

My body will rest in safety.

For you will not leave my soul among the dead,

nor let your beloved know decay.

The apostles applied these words to the Risen Lord. Towards him we resolutely set our faces.

At your right hand happiness for ever.

PERSONAL WITNESS
Psalm 65:1-7, 16, 20

The Lord sent out seventy-two disciples in pairs to prepare towns and villages for his coming. Seventy-two probably represents the number of different nations recognised at that time. May we not also see a global symbolism in the thirty-six pairs covering the three hundred and sixty degrees of the compass? The instruction of the Lord is more about the witness of their lifestyle than the content of their words. Going in pairs would witness to fraternal co-operation. They were to trust in others to support them. Their approach and greetings should exude peace.

Isaiah, in the first reading, is sensuously lyrical in singing of the return to Jerusalem after the humiliation of exile. The psalm calls us to *cry out with joy to God, sing to the glory of his name, render him glorious praise.* Initially the psalmist recalls the deeds of the past, particularly in crossing the waters dry-shod. Then he invites people to *come and hear* what God means personally to him.

Some critics say that Christianity is guilt-ridden and kill-joy. Christian mission is counter-productive unless it shows the face of love, joy and peace, the first three fruits of the Spirit. The poet, e.e. cummings, wrote that he would rather learn from one bird how to sing than teach a thousand stars how not to dance. The witness of personal peace and joy in the Lord is more attractive than a month of moral denunciations.

Come and see the works of God.
Come and hear what he did for my soul.

LAMENTATION
Psalm 68:14, 17, 30-31, 33-34, 36-37

These verses are from a long psalm of lamentation which begins in terrible distress ... *the waters have risen to my neck, there is no foothold* ... and ends in assurance of God's help. The psalmist clings to God in faith and trust.

In your great love, answer me, O God,
with your help that never fails.

The lamentation psalms have been the source of confidence to troubled souls down the ages. Brian Keenan, in his book, *An Evil Cradling*, described the consolation which the psalms gave him and his fellow captive, John MacCarthy, during their captivity in Beirut. In his dark dungeon Keenan developed a fascination with the blind harpist, Turlogh O'Carolan. In his novel called *Turlogh*, he returned to the consolation of the psalms . The tortured soul of the musician found affinity with the psalmist's pleas for redemption and liberation from suffering. The psalms' resolution in joy and praise convinced the musician of eventual happiness.

The mugged traveller in Jesus' parable, thrown in the ditch, might well have prayed: *As for me in my poverty and pain, let your help, O God, lift he up.* Priest and Levite passed him by, but help came from an unexpected source, a detested Samaritan. The Lord hears the cry of the poor and his answer may come in a way not expected. As the Irish proverb puts it: God's help is closer than the door.

'The Word is near to you, it is in your mouth and in your heart for your observance'

I will praise God's name with a song,
I will glorify him with thanksgiving.

OPEN WELCOME
Psalm 14:2-5

Abraham and Martha had the privilege of welcoming the Lord into their homes. We need not envy their privilege for all of us can have the doors of our lives open to welcome the Lord. As Saint Paul says in today's second reading, the exciting secret of our religion is Christ among us, our hope of glory. Elsewhere he wrote that our bodies are God's temples.

Psalm 14 is a song of pilgrims ascending the hill before entering the temple. They ask, *Lord, who shall dwell on your holy mountain?* The remainder of the psalm is a challenging examination of conscience which is as valid today as in the past.

How can one *walk without fault?* Certain qualities are listed in the psalm. For starters, we must act with justice and do no wrong to another. Then our speech must be truthful and our tongues never sullied by slander or slurs about our neighbour. We should avoid *godless* company, situations or reading likely to harm our faith: while honouring the good influence of *those who fear the Lord.* We should have the integrity to keep our pledges, our promises, our vows in marriage or religious commitment. The psalm highlights the injustice of cashing in on another's misfortune and of accepting bribes which prejudice the rights of the innocent.

Every day of life we are opening or closing our doors on the presence of the Lord in the way that we live. The response to the psalm repeats the key message: *The just will live in the presence of the Lord.*

GRATITUDE
Psalm 137:1-3, 6-8

Prayer takes many forms. Abraham bargains with God, as if beating down the price with a street vendor. Jesus teaches us to pray as children to the Father with persistence and absolute confidence. Knitting these readings together is a psalm of gratitude.

I thank you for your faithfulness and love
which excel all we ever knew of you.

Gratitude is at the heart of prayer. It arises from the gracious awareness of what God has given. Thanksgiving responds to the gift: praise moves beyond the gift and responds to the giver. The psalmist gives thanks, then blesses, then adores.

It is impossible to appreciate the Eucharist without a deep sense of gratitude. The very word *Eucharist* comes from the Greek word for thanking. In the Eucharist we join with the angels in adoring the thrice holy God. Liturgy is like somebody rapt in enjoyment of a great orchestra, secretly envious of the musicians who are part of the symphony. Then an angel comes, places an instrument in the hands of the spectator with the invitation to play. The person protests his inability. 'Oh no,' says the angel, 'this is different. The conductor is Jesus and if you keep your eye on him, every note you play will be part of the harmony.' That is how it is with divine liturgy. We lift up our hearts, join with the orchestra of angels and saints, in unison with Jesus our conductor, returning all praise and thanks to the Father.

Before the angels I will bless you.
I will adore before your holy temple.

WISDOM OF HEART
Psalm 89:3-6, 12-14, 17

A student asked his master, 'What does enlightenment mean?'
'I know I am going to die.'
'But everybody knows that.'
'Yes, but not everybody lives with the knowledge.'

Make us know the shortness of our life
that we may know wisdom of heart.

In biblical language, the opposite of the wise person is a fool, one who denies the existence of God. 'Fool', is what God calls the man who amassed a great fortune but forgot about his soul. 'A man's life is not made secure by what he owns.' The author of Ecclesiastes wrote of the transitory nature of every possession, accomplishment or pursuit. Paul told the Colossians to focus on the real meaning of life which is revealed in Christ.

To your eyes a thousand years are life yesterday, come and gone,
no more than a watch in the night.

As fleeting as a dream, as transitory as the grass, is the span of human life in comparison with God's eternity.

Yet the wisdom of being in touch with eternity also has an awareness that today, this tiny twenty-four hours of eternity, is a precious gift from God.

In the morning, fill us with your love;
we shall exult and rejoice all our days.

The psalmist, writing before people had developed a clear belief in life after death, is resolved to make the most of each day with God's help.

Let the favour of the Lord be upon us,
give success to the work of our hands.

CHOSEN
Psalm 32:1, 12, 18-20, 22

Happy are the people the Lord has chosen as his own.

We are a chosen people. Chosen to be. Out of the countless people who might have been conceived in my parents' loving union, one seed was fertilised. I was chosen to be. 'I thank you Lord for the wonder of my being'.

And chosen to receive the light of faith. As a cradle Christian I may not appreciate that faith is a gift of God's grace. The second reading celebrates the blessings that flow from faith. 'Only faith can guarantee the blessings that we hope for or prove the existence of the realities that at present remain unseen.'

Jesus speaks in the gospel of the blessing of being one of his chosen flock: 'There is no need to be afraid, little flock, for it has pleased your Father to give you the kingdom.'

Our psalm today gives us the phrases of prayer to show our appreciation of being chosen and blessed by God.

Ring out your joy to the Lord, O you just;
for praise is fitting for loyal hearts.

'To use God is to kill him', wrote an ancient mystic. Practice of the prayer of praise raises up the mind beyond self-centred concerns and liberates the heart.

The psalmist leads us forward in joyful anticipation of further favours from God.

Our soul is waiting for the Lord.
The Lord is our help and our shield.
May your love be upon us, O Lord,
as we place all our hope in you.

HE STOOPED DOWN
Psalm 39:2-4, 18

Sveltana, daughter of Josef Stalin, the Russian dictator, found redemption in the psalms of suffering. She was deeply depressed and thinking of imitating her mother's suicide, when a friend introduced her to the psalms. There she found the words that expressed all her pain, anxiety, rejection, despair and worthlessness: but it was pain seen in the larger context of a God who liberates and redeems.

There is a liberating honesty in the psalms. If the psalmist wants to complain to God he does not hesitate to do so. But it is always the complaint of someone who expects better, and the complaint is quickly followed by complete confidence in God. In fact, in most instances the psalmist anticipates God's favourable answer and moves forward to praising God.

In today's liturgy, we hear of Jeremiah rejected and sinking in the mud of a deep well. The responding psalm would have been the appropriate prayer in the situation.

I waited, I waited for the Lord ...
He drew me from the deadly pit,
from the miry clay.

The psalmist describes how God *stooped down* to him and *heard his cry*. In the light of the incarnation we can see the literal fulfilment of how God stooped down. Jesus entered into the miry clay of rejection, the baptismal well of suffering.

Total confidence in God puts a new song into the mouth of the psalmist ... *praise of our God*. His final prayer of trust is familiar to us in another translation:

O God, come to our aid,
O Lord, make haste to help us.

FIDELITY
Psalm 116

This is by far the shortest of the psalms but its outreach is wide, first in terms of geography, and then in terms of time. Geographically, it reaches out to all nations and peoples. This universal embrace connects with the theme of the first reading and the gospel. People from east and west, from north and south are called to take their places in the kingdom. As long as the Christian message is exclusively identified with one particular culture, there is an obstacle to the mission. Acknowledging this problem brings the challenge to rediscover the kernel of the message in a fresh and exciting way.

In relation to time, the psalm takes the long view in recognising the faithful, enduring love of God. *Strong is his love for us; he is faithful for ever.* In the Old Testament, fidelity is one of the most admired characteristics of God's love. God is love, St John assures us, so God never ceases to love. God's love is not until further notice or on condition that nothing changes. Strong love is 'always ready to excuse, to trust, to hope and to endure whatever comes.'

In the shifting sands of today's culture, people lack staying power. Our minds are opened up to many alternatives. Worldwide travel is relatively cheap. We find it harder to pin ourselves down to a definite commitment which closes the door on other possibilities. We change jobs, houses and partners. Self-assertion replaces fidelity of promise to another. But the door to salvation is narrow. The way demands choice, commitment and fidelity.

Strong is his love for us; he is faithful for ever.

A HOME FOR THE POOR
Psalm 67:4-7, 10-11

These are verses from a long psalm composed for a procession to the temple with the Ark of the Covenant. The ark was a richly decorated chest containing precious memorabilia of the exodus from slavery and the covenant enacted with Moses. The ark was a sign of the presence of God's protecting power in their midst.

The just shall rejoice at the presence of God.

During the procession, people chanted a long list of God's deeds. Whereas our creed today commences with belief in God as creator, the Jews thought of God primarily as a God who saves. God who rescued them from bondage in Egypt continued to save and rescue people from various plights. A litany of favours was chanted in the procession. God is *father of the orphan, defender of the widow.* Widows and orphans were extremely vulnerable in the days when women held no property rights.

Today's first reading calls for gentleness and humility in dealing with people, pointing out that pride is an evil growth. In the gospel Jesus reminds those who are wealthy enough to host parties not to forget the poor, the crippled, the lame and the blind. These were the very people who were considered to be excluded from the messianic banquet. 'That they cannot pay you back means that payment will be made to you when the virtuous rise again.' The Christian view is that the poor are the door-keepers of heaven for the rich.

In your goodness, O God, you prepared a home for the poor.

COST AND VALUE
Psalm 89:3-6, 12-14, 17

Wisdom is the theme linking the first reading, psalm and gospel today. In the words of the first reading, wisdom enables the mind to know the intentions of God and to divine the will of the Lord. Wisdom lifts one up to see things in God's vast timespan.

To your eyes a thousand years
are like yesterday, come and gone,
no more than a watch in the night.

How is wisdom connected with today's gospel? Great crowds accompanied Jesus, but he challenged them on the depth and sincerity of their following. He presented two parables on the cost of true discipleship. A pessimist is inhibited by the cost, but the optimist is liberated by the value. Jesus valued the grace of discipleship as even greater than the precious ties of family love. Following him on the way to the cross would be costly to self-centred pursuits: but wisdom would discern the value.

Make us know the shortness of our life
that we may gain wisdom of heart.

Wisdom can evaluate matters in the long term view but it also discerns the presence of God in each day. After reflecting on the thousand year timespan, the psalmist prays that the little twenty-four hours of time which is today would be blessed with God's love, joy and favour.

In the morning, fill us with your love;
we shall exult and rejoice all our days.
Let the favour of the Lord be upon us:
give success to the work of our hands.

Wisdom is the crowning virtue among the gifts of the Holy Spirit.

REMEMBERING MERCY
Psalm 50:3-4, 12-13, 17-19

This is a rare Sunday when the three readings share a common theme. God's mercy was shown to Moses, to Paul and to the sinners who were drawn to the company of Jesus. The *Miserere* psalm is one of the most heartfelt prayers ever composed, expressing at once the sinner's humble sorrow and the praise of God's mercy.

Have mercy on me, God, in your kindness.

We can hear its sentiments giving direction to the steps of the Prodigal Son. He decides to leave the land of famine when he remembers his father's house where mercy, kindness and compassion were valued. This uplifting memory gives renewed hope to his crushed spirit. He needs a total cleansing so he prays for *a pure heart and a steadfast spirit.* He will humbly confess his sin against God and family. All he can offer his father is a humbled, contrite heart. His wasted body pleads:

Do not cast me away from your presence
nor deprive me of your holy spirit.

Far from casting sinners away from his presence, Jesus was a scandal in the way he welcomed sinners, and even shared food with them. Paul, in the second reading, gives his personal experience: 'Christ Jesus came into the world to save sinners. I myself am the greatest of them.' On the cross he took sin on himself that we might be justified before God.

This age-old psalm continues to provide the language of prayer to the crushed heart. And it goes beyond sorrow to the praise of God.

O Lord, open my lips,
and my mouth shall declare your praise.

BLESSED ARE THE POOR
Psalm 112:1-2, 4-8

Today's readings carry a severe warning to the rich but the psalm gives hope to the poor. Amos lists a variety of ways in which injustices are done to the poor but he warns that nothing escapes the eye of God. 'Never will I forget a single thing you have done.'

Care for the poor and downtrodden is one of the great themes of Luke's gospel. 'He has filled the hungry with good things, the rich he sent empty away.' In the follow-up to the parable of the astute steward, Jesus warns that money is tainted with temptation and easily enslaves the owner. But, on the other hand, it affords one the opportunity to help the poor who, in turn, will form heaven's welcoming committee.

The psalm exhorts *us to praise the Lord, who raises the poor*. God is pictured *high above all nations, above the heavens his glory*. Yet, so great is the compassion of God for the poor that he *stoops from the heights to look down, to look down upon heaven and earth*. The psalmist would have been surprised at the extent of this coming down of God in the poverty of the incarnation, what Paul called the self-emptying of Christ.

From the dust he lifts up the lowly,
from the dungheap he raises the poor.

A conscientious decision to work for justice at the side of the poor is more than an optional extra for a Christian. Without that commitment, prayer runs the risk of being an escape from harsh reality.

Praise the Lord, who raises the poor.

SINS OF NEGLECT
Psalm 145:6-10

Today's first reading and gospel are about sins of neglect. Amos upbraids those who are smugly ensconced in luxury while 'about the ruin of Joseph they do not care at all'. This refers to the sin of the sons of Jacob who did not directly murder Joseph, their brother, but simply left him in a well to perish.

Jesus tells the parable of the rich man whose sin was in neglecting the poor man at his gate. Lazarus, poor, hungry, lacking medical care, and unjustly treated is the personification of Luke's four beatitudes. The rich man personifies the four woes. The only person in any parable to be given a name is Lazarus, meaning God-has-compassion.

The day's psalm celebrates this compassion of God. Three times we repeat *it is the Lord,* words of recognition used by the beloved disciple when the risen Lord came to them at the lakeside. *It is the Lord* who is present in the compassionate activities of those who work for justice, feed the hungry, liberate the oppressed and care for the neglected people of our society. 'Where charity and love dwell, there is God.'

Sins of omission are easily overlooked. Self-serving piety comfortably launders conscience of its social responsibilities. 'It is better to have a tender heart at home than to burn incense at a distant shrine' (Chinese proverb). Charity has to be proactive, looking beyond self, taking the initiative, making the gesture, doing what is possible. *It is the Lord* who inspires the work of those who work for justice and the alleviation of poverty. Through their concern, *the Lord will reign for ever.*

FAITHFUL
Psalm 94:1-2, 6-9

This psalm is used in the Prayer of the Church as a wake-up call at the start of Morning Prayer. Is an invitation and a warning. We are invited to *come ... ring out our joy ... give thanks ... and kneel before the God who made us.* We are reminded that *he is our God* and that we are a chosen people, *the flock that is led by his hand.*

The invitation then turns to a warning not to rest on past privileges but to continue to *listen to his voice today.* The psalmist reminds us of a time when the chosen people listened more to their inner doubts than to God's promise of protection. *Massah* means strife, recalling how they rebelled against Moses. *Meribah* means testing, no longer being sure of God's promise, lacking the sort of faith that would persevere in darkness.

The prophet Habakkuk answered the people who were complaining that God was not answering their prayer to be delivered from unjust oppression.

'See how he flags, he whose soul is not at rights,

but the upright man will live by his faithfulness.'

The gospel picks up the theme of faithfulness. 'Increase our faith,' the apostles ask. The Lord replied in the parable of the servant who is faithful in his duties regardless of whether he gets a special reward or not. To become faith-full one must strive to be faithful.

O that today you would listen to his voice!
Harden not your hearts.

GRATITUDE
Psalm 97:1-4

Sing a new song to the Lord
for he has worked wonders.

Chesterton once wrote that the world is not lacking in wonders but in wonderment. An old Irish proverb says that what is rare is wonderful, the implication being that the wonder of what is familiar or commonplace is often overlooked. The psalmist reminds us of the wonders of God's *salvation, justice, truth and love,* which never grow stale. They call for a response in a fresh appreciation and new song each day.

The everyday miracles of life are too easily taken for granted. Good health is most appreciated by those who have had it threatened. I like the way that Luke describes how the leper, going along the road, found himself cured. Did he ever find the gift of health in the days before his affliction? Having found God's favour, he turned back on the road, praising God at the top of his voice and thanking Jesus in a gesture of humble prostration.

Only one out of the ten who were cured turned back in gratitude. Is that our average score in showing appreciation to God and to people? Gratitude begins in finding, seeing, appreciating what others have done. It means a lot. Negative words stab our confidence and bleed it to death. How many priests have dried up because of lack of affirmation? How many marriages would flourish if partners showed appreciation?

Gratitude never grows stale because it is generated by a gracious sense of wonder. Each day it begets *a new song to the Lord.*

THE LORD IS YOUR GUARD
Psalm 120

We get a complete psalm today, something that doesn't happen too often. And what a beautiful prayer of trust it is!

Our help is in the name of the Lord
who made heaven and earth.

The theme of the day is expressed in the opening line of the gospel: to pray continually and not to lose heart. As long as Moses held his arms aloft in prayer, victory was theirs: but when his arms fell, the military advantage swung the other way.

The psalmist is on a journey, probably a pilgrimage to the temple. He describes how he lifts up his eyes to the mountains. In this instance he is not admiring their majesty or beauty, but he sees them as towering problems to be surmounted. But not to worry ... *my help shall come from the Lord who made heaven and earth*. Six times the word *guard* is used to express how God is with us night and day, above us and below us, protecting from evil, from sunstroke and moonstroke, on every step of life's pilgrimage. It reminds one of St Patrick's Breastplate.

The Lord says to pray continually and not to lose heart. This beautiful prayer is very suitable at the beginning of a journey or on a visit to a hospital patient. And it provides a consoling line of prayer regularly used at the final journey of the deceased to the church.

The Lord will guard your going and coming
both now and forever.

HUMBLE PRAYER
Psalm 33:2-3, 17-19, 23

This is the fourth successive Sunday when the extract from Luke concerns some quality of prayer. Today the emphasis is on humility.

Psalm 33 is one of those alphabetical compositions in which the each succeeding letter of the Hebrew alphabet is used to begin a verse. The three verses selected for today's liturgy match the humble contrition of the tax collector which is contrasted with the boastfulness of the Pharisee in the Lord's parable.

The attitude of the Pharisee is proud and arrogant while his prayer is boastful. But there is a wry observation that he said these words to himself. In contrast, as the first reading says, the prayer of the humble person pierces the clouds. The tax collector recognises that he is a sinner with nothing to boast about. But he trusts in the mercy of God. 'God, be merciful to me, a sinner.' If he were to boast it would be about God, not himself.

In the Lord my soul shall make its boast,
the humble shall hear and be glad.

The psalmist has experienced injustice but he is confident that the justice of God will prevail.

The just call and the Lord hears
and rescues them in their distress.

The tax collector was rescued and justified by the Lord's mercy for he went home at rights with God. Merely recognising one's unworthiness would destroy hope, but when the awareness of personal unworthiness is balanced with belief in God's merciful goodness, then humility flourishes. It nurtures a prayer to pierce the clouds.

The Lord is close to the broken-hearted.

LOVER OF ALL
Psalm 144:1-2, 8-11, 13-14

The first reading, from Wisdom, calls God the Lord, the lover of life. 'You love all that exists, you hold nothing of what you have made in abhorrence, for had you hated anything, you would not have formed it.' Having loved us in creation, God's love remains faithful, unending. Today's gospel closes with the statement that the Son of Man came to seek out and save what was lost. Zacchaeus was a case in point. His outward wealth could not camouflage his inner sense of being lost. When Jesus looked at him and spoke to him, joy entered his life.

The psalm chosen to accompany these readings is an alphabetical composition. It begins with blessing the Lord.

I will give you glory, O God my King
I will bless your name for ever.

Then we hear a litany of the favours experienced by those who enjoy God's friendship. We are invited to give glory, to bless, to praise and to thank God who is kind and full of compassion, slow to anger, abounding in love. Furthermore, the love of God never ceases, for *the Lord is faithful in all his words and loving in all his deeds.* Seven times the word *all* occurs in these verses. God is lover of all.

When Jesus went to the house of Zacchaeus there were some who complained that he had gone to stay with a sinner. But the all-embracing love of God has a special concern for sinners.

The Lord supports all who fall
and raises up all who are bowed down.

THE SIGHT OF YOUR GLORY
Psalm 16:1, 5-6, 8, 15

The psalmist has been the victim of injustice. He pleads that he is entitled to God's justice for *I have kept my feet firmly in your paths; there was no faltering in my steps.* The psalm has two moving images of protection. *Guard me as the apple of your eye* ... with that instinctive reaction one would use to protect the eye from harm. *Hide me under the shelter of your wings* ... like the mother hen gathering her chicks under her wing. The psalmist is confident that God's answer will be there, first post, when he wakes up in the morning.

As for me, in my justice I shall see your face
and be filled, when I awake, with the sight of your glory.

In the light of our Christian belief, this response becomes a sigh of longing for the beatific vision. In the confusion of ideas today, many people have accepted the Saducees belief that there is no life after death: some opt for a hazy idea of an impersonal unity with the cosmos, while others speak of reincarnation, coming back in this life on a higher or lower level, depending on the cleansing of one's karma. Christian belief is so much more noble: enjoying the beatific vision ... 'the same as the angels,' as Jesus said, 'children of the resurrection, children of God.' Paul writes of 'such inexhaustible hope and sure comfort.'

A beautiful, November prayer to be recited in the name of our departed friends:

I shall be filled when I awake with the sight of your glory.

ORCHESTRA OF PRAISE
Psalm 97:5-9

Today's readings offer two ways of thinking about the end of life: as a dreaded time of destruction or as a joyful liberation. Malachi warns that the day of retribution is coming for the arrogant. The gospel of the day also speaks of a coming day of destruction. But, according to Malachi, for the God-fearing, the sun will shine out with healing in its rays.

It is the theme of celebration which is picked up in the psalm, which is part of a song for the enthronement of a king. Christians look upon the final judgement as the manifestation of the reign of God over all creation.

The Lord comes to rule the peoples with fairness.

The enthronement calls for music. The orchestra is huge. People are asked to raise their voices in song to the accompaniment of harp, trumpets and horn. Then the orchestra of all creation joins in. As a popular song put it, all God's creatures have a place in the choir. Listen to the thundering crescendo as the mighty sea crashes on the rocks. And then the mood is pianissimo as we hear the playful child-river tripping merrily over the stones to the rhythm of clapping hands. The hills echo the music. The great occasion is the coming of the Lord.

For the Lord comes,
he comes to rule the earth.

Christian hope looks forward to the resurrection of the dead and life everlasting. In the meantime, get into training for heaven by praising the Lord with joy.

JOURNEY'S END
Psalm 121:1-5

I wonder was the repentant thief familiar with the psalms. If he was, he might have thought of today's response when Jesus promised him a place in paradise.

I rejoiced when I heard them say:
'Let us go to God's house.'

Today's psalm was composed for the end of the pilgrims' journey to Jerusalem. The aching muscles were soon forgotten in the joy that their feet were at last standing within the gates of Jerusalem. We can imagine how pilgrims from rural areas stood in admiration of the well fortified city.

Jerusalem is built as a city
strongly compact.

This was the place chosen by David, as a centre of unity for the diverse tribes, in the hope that their rivalries would be healed in celebrating their shared calling as the chosen people.

It is there that the tribes go up,
the tribes of the Lord.

Its name meant the city of *shalom*, peace. It was to be a holy city, a place of pilgrimage. It was the supreme joy of any Jew's heart to sing the praises of God's name in the temple.

At the end of the church's liturgical journey, our thoughts turn to the end of life's pilgrimage. The aches and blisters of the road are healed at the glimpse of the city where our king reigns, inviting us to enter eternal paradise.

I rejoiced when I heard them say:
'Let us go to God's house.'

STRONG AND FAITHFUL
Psalm 116

This may be the shortest of the psalms, but it is long in outreach to all nations and peoples. Rightly then is it chosen as the psalm for missionaries. Today it is a prayer of gratitude for the missionary zeal of Patrick and others who brought the message of Christ to our land. He lit a fire for Christ at the western extreme of the world. By the grace of God, the Irish in turn became intrepid missionaries to other countries. We praise God through this psalm for the faithful Irish men and women who brought the light of faith to people in many lands, not only in word, but in education, health-care and service to the poor and hungry.

God's love is strong and faithful. These qualities could also be found in the life of Patrick. Patrick's love for Christ and his message proved stronger than any resentment he may have felt towards the people who had held him in captivity. The source of this strong love was constant prayer. He wrote: 'The love of God and his fear came to me more and more, and my faith was strengthened.' This strong love nurtured in him the fidelity to persevere in the face of problems. He wrote of twelve dangers in which his life was at stake, but God always protected him, at times forewarning him of the dangers.

Ireland has changed hugely in recent years. On the feast of Patrick, we pray that we will remain strong in love and faithful to the way of Christ.

IN GOLD OF OPHIR
Psalm 44:10-12, 16

Since the Second Vatican Council, devotion to Mary has been enriched by considering her as the mother and model of the church. What God bestowed on her shows what God intends for the church. Today's Preface celebrates her assumption as 'the beginning and pattern of the church in its perfection, and a sign of sure hope and comfort for your people on their pilgrim way.'

The psalm of the day was composed for a royal wedding. It is one of those psalms which acquired a new level of meaning, like water changed into wine, at the coming of Christ. Paul called the church the bride of Christ. This psalm now celebrates how Christ will take the church and make her holy and spotless as his heavenly bride.

What is Mary's role in this wedding? In today's gospel she is identified by Elizabeth as the mother of the Lord. She is the Queen Mother to whom we can apply the words of the psalm: *On your right stands the queen, in gold of Ophir.* That highest quality Arabian gold signifies the glory of Mary at her Son's side in heaven. In ancient royalties the Queen Mother was far more influential than the young king's bride-queen. She whispers advice to the new bride: *Listen, O daughter, give ear to my words: forget your own people and your father's house.*

She reminds us that our eternal home is in heaven and that we have here no lasting city. She is a sign of hope and a comfort on our pilgrim way.

ALL SAINTS
Psalm 23:1-6

Such are the people who seek your face, O Lord.

What a lovely way of describing the lives of the saints! One of my favourite prayers from the psalms is the plea: *let your face shed its light upon us.* Pope John Paul II took great delight in canonising new saints because, at a time when the scandals of the church get a lot of publicity, focusing on the saints manifests the holiness of the church.

Our psalm today is the song of pilgrims on their way to the mount of the sacred temple. Although they sing of God's presence *in all the earth and its fullness*, yet they regard the temple as the place where God is to be worshipped in a very special way. Who is worthy to enter the sacred house? Three special qualities are recognised: *clean hands*, unsoiled by unjust dealings: *pure hearts*, free of evil intentions; and a desire for God which renders every other pursuit *worthless*. Those who thus seek the face of God will be blessed and rewarded.

Today we celebrate all the saints who now enjoy the beatific vision of the face of God. In the pilgrimage of life their *clean hands* served God in practical works of charity. Their *pure hearts* were free of malice. They *desired not worthless things* but they sought God with all their hearts, minds and strength.

Such are the people who seek him,
seek the face of the God of Jacob.

A SONG OF SALVATION
Psalm 97:1-4

The immaculate conception of Mary was like the first light of dawn anticipating the appearance of its source, the sun, over the horizon. The saving deeds of Jesus were anticipated when God preserved the mother of the Saviour free from all taint of sin. She is addressed by the angel of the annunciation as being full of grace. It is a new deed, a wonder to be savoured.

Sing a new song to the Lord
for he has worked wonders.
His right hand and his holy arm
have brought salvation.

Salvation is the theme of the psalm for the feast. The fundamental concept of God for the Jews was a God who saves. The story of salvation reached its climax in Jesus, whose name means Saviour.

The Lord has made known his salvation. In the *Magnificat*, Mary proclaimed God as her Saviour, thirty-three years before the saving events took place.

He has shown his justice to the nations. Mary, sinless from her very conception, is the model of the holy justice to be attained by the church. She was chosen by God to be a headline or model of the graces of salvation. What God intends for the many he first accomplishes in the one.

He has remembered his truth and his love. She is that woman, promised long ages ago, whose offspring would crush the head of the serpent.

The holy privilege of Mary foretells the destiny of the church.
Shout aloud to the Lord,
ring out your joy.